East–West business collaboration

Corporate governance is an area of key importance for students of comparative management and international business; nowhere more so than in analyses of the post-socialist economies of the East, where both governments and enterprises have undergone major structural transformations.

While the complexities of governance in the socialist enterprises are not well understood by prospective investors in these economies, the governance of western economies is equally opaque to the post-socialist managers responsible for promoting reform. This book is designed to sensitize managers, of East and West, to the kind of governance issues they will face when working together.

An outstanding feature of *East–West Business Collaboration* is that it represents a genuine dialogue between managers, consultants and academics who have worked on both sides of the former ideological divide. The book is an invitation to practising managers, academics and consultants specializing in post-socialist economies to join in dialogue.

Max Boisot is currently Professor of Strategic Management at ESADE, Barcelona and Senior Associate at the Judge Institute of Management Studies at the University of Cambridge.

East–West business collaboration

The challenge of governance in post-socialist enterprises

Edited by Max Boisot

COS

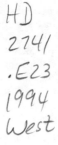

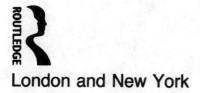

London and New York

First published 1994
by Routledge
11 New Fetter Lane, London EC4P 4EE

Simultaneously published in the USA and Canada
by Routledge
29 West 35th Street, New York, NY 10001

© 1994 Foundacion Jose Maria Anzizu (COS)

Typeset in Bembo by
J&L Composition Ltd, Filey, North Yorkshire
Printed and bound in Great Britain by
Biddles Ltd, Guildford and King's Lynn

British Library Cataloguing in Publication Data

A catalogue record for this book is available from the British Library

Library of Congress Cataloging in Publication Data has been applied for

ISBN 0–415–10269–3   ISBN 0–415–10270–7 (pbk)

Contents

Figures and exhibits

FIGURES

EXHIBITS

Tables

Contributors

Anton Artemyev has been working for three years as a professor and Deputy Director of Programmes in one of the leading Russian business schools: the International Management Institute of St Petersburg. Having moved to management consultancy in 1992, he now works for an international European-based company, SIAR-BOSSARD, heading the office in St Petersburg.

Max Boisot is Professor of Strategic Management at ESADE in Barcelona and a Senior Associate of the Judge Institute of Management at Cambridge University. From 1984 to 1988 he was Director and Dean of the China–EC Management Programme. Max Boisot has participated in World Bank missions to China and Vietnam, in UNDP missions to Albania and EC missions to Rumania. He is currently involved in the training of managers in the CIS on behalf of the EC Commission.

John Child is the Guiness Professor of Management Studies at the University of Cambridge and is also a Professorial Fellow of St. John's College, Cambridge. He was previously Dean and Director of the China–Europe Management Institute in Beijing. His interests are in the management of international business ventures, an area in which he both researches and consults.

Bob Garratt is an international strategy consultant specializing in the development of direction-givers and their strategic thinking. He is Chairman of Media Projects International in London, and of Organisational Development Ltd in Hong Kong. He is a visiting fellow at the Management School, Imperial College, London and an Associate of the Judge Institute, Cambridge University. His books include 'The Learning Organisation', 'Learning to Lead' and 'China Business Briefing'.

Livia Markoczy is researching at the Judge Institute of Management Studies, University of Cambridge. She is also a faculty member of the Budapest University of Economics, from which she received her doctorate. Her interests are in the cognitive aspects of managerial learning within internationally mixed-management organizations.

Jan-Peter Paul is Visiting Professor at the European Institute of Public Administration (EIPA) in Maastricht, Holland. He has had more than twenty years professional experience from international business and management competence development. He has worked extensively in Eastern and Central Europe, including Russia, during the past ten years, and is Director of the Helsinki Institute. He is multilingual (in five languages) and has published more than forty books and other publications.

Ian Turner has been at Henley Management College since 1984 where he is Lead Tutor in Strategy. He is responsible for managing the College's links with Russia, which involves supporting Henley's partner in St. Petersburg. His current research interests include work on strategy and structure in international companies, which involves extensive foreign travel. Ian contributes regularly to a management journal, was previously with UMIST in Manchester and has lived and worked in Germany. He speaks fluent German and can communicate in French and Russian.

Manuel Vallejo As an international manager (1980–1992), Manuel Vallejo has specialized in setting up subsidiaries in lesser developed countries such as Ecuador, Peru, Venezuela; and joint ventures in countries in transition to market system, such as China and Poland. Recently moved to North Carolina, USA, he has lectured at Duke University and Davidson College. He is currently advising western firms on how to establish themselves in China. He holds an MBA from ESADE, Barcelona, and a degree in law from the Central University of Barcelona.

Foreword

It is with great pleasure that I write these words to present this book after COS's third Round Table.

Since it was founded in 1989, COS's main activity has been to organize an annual meeting with a small number of managers, academics and consultants who openly discuss a topic of interest related to the management of organizations. In 1991, after two years of discussing cultural and organizational aspects of mergers and acquisitions, we decided to take the risk of exploring issues related to East–West business collaboration. I must say that the experience was much more challenging, interesting and rewarding than any of our prior expectations. The reason for this success is due, as always, to a number of individuals who brought their expertise, enthusiasm and unselfish collaboration to the project. First of all our Chairman, Max Boisot, and secondly the managers, academics and consultants who participated in the meeting, especially those who have contributed to this book with cases or articles.

To all of them, on behalf of the Board of COS, my sincere thanks and appreciation. We all hope that this book, as well as other COS activities, will contribute in the development of organizations that are more efficient in economic as well as in social and human terms.

José M. de Anzizu
Director General, COS

Introduction

Governance is a word that is much in vogue these days. A failure of governance, for example, is given as an explanation for the poor performance of many UK enterprises, the scandals on the Japanese stock markets, BCCI, and so on. The term is also cheerfully confused with management and corporate strategy. It is, in effect, in danger of being made to cover so much of organizational life that it will end up covering nothing.

Governance is, in effect, a cybernetic concept describing the feedback and control mechanisms by which a system, *any* system, keeps itself oriented towards the purpose for which it was conceived. As such, it can apply to nation states, to military organizations, commercial enterprises, or more metaphysically perhaps, to individuals (why are we here?, etc.).

The collapse of communism in Eastern Europe – and, since the COS⋆ Round Table, in the Soviet Union – is no less than the breakdown of a governance structure on a massive scale and at multiple levels. Governance at the political level establishes the scope for governance at the enterprise level and, where the two are closely intertwined, if the first collapses, the second must follow. By implication, the reconstructing of the first entails that of the latter.

Surprisingly, problems of governance hardly rate a mention in western discussions of enterprise reforms in post-communist

⋆ The Centre for Organisational Studies (COS) is sponsored by the Foundation José M. de Anzizu and has the specific brief to encourage and develop projects, encounters, conferences and research in the organizational field, whilst keeping in mind the intercultural and interdisciplinary issues involved, as well as the need to link theories with their practical applications. COS is based in Barcelona, Spain, but its vocation – as shown in the composition of its Board – is international. Each year, COS organises a Round Table in a different European city. In June of 1991, the choice was Warsaw.

countries. The market is the solvent that will take care of all problems 'internal' to the firm. Privatize first, and let the self-regulating power of market forces take care of the rest.

The fact that the self-regulating power of markets *itself* depends on the effectiveness with which its signals embed themselves into the feedback and control systems – i.e. in governance structures – of economic agents, is either not noticed or passed over in silence.

For its third annual Round Table, COS decided to address this oversight and to examine the problems of corporate governance in post-communist enterprises in particular insofar as they affect the ability of such enterprises to collaborate with western, market-oriented firms and hence to integrate into the world economy.

Because this Round Table was to be more of an 'experiential' learning exercise than one of pure reflection (for more on this, see below) it was decided to hold it in the heartland of the post-communist revolution: Poland. The site chosen was the village of Monralin, located 25 kilometres outside Warsaw in a retreat belonging to the Polish Academy of Sciences, a pleasant cluster of 1920s two-storey brick buildings discreetly tucked away inside a small secluded wood.

The participants, with one exception, were European – eastern, central, western – although one was currently working in the People's Republic of China and another in Hong Kong. As with other COS Round Tables, a balance was struck between academics (the theory builders), consultants (those who apply the theories) and practising managers (those who have to endure the application of theories).

This strange alchemy, distilled out of a multicultural, multi-occupational brew, exercised its own effect over the three days.

The lingua franca of the Round Table was English. In the event, the use of English presented no great problem to the non-native speaker participants. Were there communication difficulties? Surprisingly few, considering the opportunities for them. Those which did arise were non-linguistic; cultural and temperamental perhaps, caused by lack of shared experience, knowledge, and priorities. Given the mix of managers (mainly from Eastern Europe), academics and consultants (mainly from the West), there may have been some frustration on the part of the eastern participants over the immediate applicability of theoretical models to the urgent and concrete situations they were confronting. At the outset at least, the managers seemed to see themselves as each coming from a particular country with a particular communist and post-communist history, and therefore, with a set of problems that were unique. They expected them to be treated as such. By the end of the Round Table, however, there was somewhat more identification between the easterners, a feeling that they were not all in entirely separate boats. The western academics may have started out with the impression that any learning that occurred during the Round Table would primarily flow from west to east, and no doubt did. However, there was also general recognition that the West had a lot to learn, too. It may also have been that a number (certainly not all) of the eastern managers were too immersed in their day-to-day struggles simply to survive to reflect upon or to appreciate the finer considerations of long-term organizational growth and the more subtle features of a market economy. Yet despite their different backgrounds and primary interests, the participants in the Round Table were well able to exchange information and experience and this on a level that went well beyond the superficial.

The idea of holding the Round Table in Eastern Europe aimed at more than a mere symbolic gesture, important as this might be for a foundation eager to be relevant as well as scholarly. This was COS's first attempt at linking its Round Table theme to a live and concrete issue. In March 1991, as chairman designate of the Round Table, I had come to Poland to write a case study on a small private enterprise called Sportis which was having difficulties coping with the turbulence that the reforms had been generating since 1989. My idea had been that the Round Table would take this case study as its point of departure, would invite its senior managers, Thomas Holç and Michal Syski, to take part in the proceedings as active contributors, and would offer a field trip to the firm's premises to all participants. The Sportis case was never intended to be the focus of the Round Table, but rather the point around which other themes and discussions would crystallize. All participants had experience and knowledge to contribute and, indeed, many brought their own case studies with them. Sportis, however, provided a live experience against which other live experiences could be contrasted and assessed.

It might be asked, why choose a small private company in Poland when so many large, state-owned enterprises are going under for lack of adequate governance? Would not a larger firm have been more relevant to the topic? Two replies:

1 Socialist, state-owned enterprises have been much studied whereas private firms in a socialist society have gone almost

unnoticed. Yet they have been around in a number of socialist countries – Hungary, Yugoslavia, the PRC, Poland – for over a decade.

2 Small private firms may turn out to offer a much better return on western reform efforts than the bloated and geriatric state-owned firms currently languishing in intensive care. For all the difficulties faced by the Polish economy, its private sector grew by nearly 50 per cent in 1990 alone, and in as resolutely Marxist a country as the People's Republic of China, the private sector – which now for all practical purposes includes collective enterprises – currently accounts for 50 per cent of total industrial output. In Vietnam, another ideological diehard, the figure is even higher.

   It would be dangerous to assume, given such figures, that the problem of governance in post-socialist economies necessarily reduces to that of state-owned firms. If either China's or Vietnam's private sectors successfully maintain their current growth rates, then by the year 2000 a larger part of their economies will end up in private hands than they currently do in France or Spain, and this in card-carrying communist economies that still intend to maintain a state-owned sector no matter what it costs them.

Thus, looking at the problems of governance in a small private firm does more than just plug isolated gaps in our knowledge of socialist economies; it effectively focuses on an area which in future years will need at least as much attention, if not more, than the moribund state-owned sector that policy-makers, east and west, are so busy nursing today.

From the start of the Round Table, the atmosphere was good. The participants gave lengthy, relaxed and quite personal self-introductions, which set the tone for the following days. The group then got down to the task of identifying the problems it wanted to air: the difficulty of finding suitably qualified managers in Eastern Europe; establishing who owns what and how to deal with the obstructiveness of the *nomenklatura* still surviving within firms; the jealousy between state-owned and private enterprises as well as between the various post-communist countries; the difference in corporate culture and values of small as opposed to large enterprises; information feedback and organizational learning systems; and so on. This process of problem identification was not confined to the first session alone, but went on for the duration of the Round Table. Certainly, at all times there were always more questions raised than answers suggested. The problem areas, however, gradually became more focused as time went by.

To what extent Sportis would dominate the sessions was left open for participants to decide; in fact, the company and its problems provided a leitmotif throughout the Round Table proceedings, and linked together the various presentations. Since these ranged from accounts of vastly differing joint ventures (see the contributions by Jan-Peter Paul, Anton Artemyev and Ian Turner, Manuel Vallejo and Max Boisot) to academic models of governance and organizational learning (see contributions by John Child and Livia Markoczy, Bob Garratt and Max Boisot), having Sportis as a case at hand – and having the management of Sportis physically at hand as well – was, in retrospect, what gave the Round Table much of its coherence.

It soon became apparent that the Round Table did not see Sportis's problems the way the Sportis representatives that were present did. As far as the latter were concerned, the firm's biggest internal problem centred around its workers. These tended to be perceived by the Sportis management as lazy, inefficient, and unmotivated; they had no interest in their work, or in the welfare of the company. Neither the promise of better pay nor the threat of dismissal had any apparent effect on their behaviour. Since qualified staff (supervisors) were almost impossible to find, and since the productivity of the Sportis workforce was only around half that of workers in other countries, Sportis was extremely worried about its future competitiveness in the open market. This led naturally to the second major problem: the finding of markets, and the need to build up relationships with suitable partners/customers. Unlike other participants, Sportis managers saw no great problem in dealing with the USSR but were worried about payment now that the clearing rouble had been dumped.

This examination of how Sportis should go about working out a strategy led to more general discussions on topics which kept recurring for the duration of the Round Table: survival versus growth strategies, the nature of a joint venture, etc. A company such as Sportis which is struggling to keep its head above water appears to be in no position to become strategically autonomous. It is fundamentally dependent; dependent on its customers, on its subcontractors, and on any prospective joint venture partners.

Customers can dictate their terms – in the case of Sportis, for example, they can and do forbid it to carry out subcontracting work for their competitors. Customers with no long-term interest in the welfare of their supplier, with no commitment beyond the next contract and no concern other than low cost, hardly amount to attractive joint venture partners. Ideally, a joint venture should involve shared risks and rewards, with each partner considering the other's growth as a path to its own greater success and profit. The choice of a suitable partner is, therefore, extremely important for a firm striving to become strategically autonomous. In the case of East–West joint ventures, however, it could be that the western partner's interest will typically be shorter-term than that of the eastern partner, that it will be able to learn faster than the latter and will then lose interest in the joint venture as its ability to operate competently in its eastern partner's environment increases.

Another recurring topic throughout the Round Table centred on the social aspect of organizations. Lee Vansina's overriding concern was the welfare of the members of any given community. His worry was not so much about governance in East–West joint ventures as about the lack thereof. Individuals can respond to new opportunities much faster than can the state, and they often do so without thought to the effects on society of their initiatives. In countries without a comprehensive social system, without social legislation applicable to both the public and the private sectors, it is all the more important for organizations to be able to take care of and provide for their members. The current situation in post-communist countries is extremely discouraging in this respect. Where the communist state used to provide a high degree of social security, there is now a void. The situation at Sportis may be typical and hardly encouraging: if the firm's management has no answers of its own on questions of social security and, moreover, does not consider that in a market economy social security should be the concern of a small company, how can its workers be expected to cope with the ensuing insecurity? Organizational development cannot take place without some form of social provision, but the way things are going in Eastern Europe, the two are increasingly being divorced from each other. The Round Table was left wondering whether or not this is a step forward or backward in the development of the region's entrepreneurial potential.

Chapter 1

Directing and the learning board

Bob Garratt

INTRODUCTION

Governance concerns the structures within which an enterprise receives its basic orientation and direction. The collapse of communism in Eastern Europe and the Soviet Union will change the governance requirements of productive enterprises and broaden the group of stakeholders that a governance structure will be required to serve. The assumption currently made is that governance structures in post-communist economies will naturally align themselves with those currently operating in Western Europe, yet such an assumption sits oddly alongside the soul-searching that is going on today concerning the role of one of the key actors in a corporate governance structure: the company director. In this paper, we examine the issues from a UK perspective and discuss, where appropriate, their implication for enterprise reform in Eastern Europe.

THE CHANGING CONTEXTS

Two sets of pressures are combining to force directors to rethink their roles. One set, external economic, legislative, and investor pressures, will have a profound effect on who becomes a director and what he will do in future. The other set, internal pressures for developing directors' competence and organizational effectiveness, is in part a response to the external issues. Both sets are increasingly widely recognized and are helping form the context of the wider public debate on directors' pay and duties. So far, little has been said about how they can be absorbed into the normal exercise of board functions. This paper suggests some ways forward based on action research with boards.

The external pressures on boards to rethink their roles and responsibilities come from two major sources. First, in western market societies, legislative changes are creating a new account-ablility and regulatory frameworks in which directors must be seen to be more publicly responsible for exercising their function. In the UK, for example, changes in the Insolvency Act, and in the Companies Act, as well as talk of new EC laws, have focused directors' attention not just on the need to obey the letter of the new laws – previously these were more honoured in the breach – but also on the importance of honouring them in the spirit in which they were enacted. Directors' minds have been concentrated by the emergence of personal, rather than corporate, liability for their actions, although the implied exposure of home and family to one's corporate behaviour has not been fully understood by many directors. It will need to become not just understood but central to board thinking and decision taking as the exercise of directoral duties becomes more closely and publicly examined in future.

Second, the growing activism of groups of shareholders and stakeholders – customers, suppliers, local communities, and environ-mental groups (the Green issue is no longer restricted to Body Shop as IBM and ICI are seen to take public stances on it at board level) – in and around organizations is leading to a more critical public scrutiny of directors' actions. The pressure from disenchanted investors and investment managers for more 'professional' directors in Europe, the US, and even in Japan, is today a significant trend. Institutional watchdogs, for example, see signs of a more public debate on what are alleged to be underperforming boards. The demand for more transparency in the working of boards is being reinforced by governmental, Institute of Directors (IOD), Confederation of British Industry (CBI) and EC Commission rethinking on the roles and duties of directors. Such rethinking runs increasingly along the lines of 'you can run but cannot hide'. The recent Association of British Insurers report on the subject led to scare headlines of a threatened investment strike against public companies who do not have properly defined board roles and carefully selected and trained boards. Whilst these headlines were overdramatic it does seem that the pressure is on for a public debate on at least three interconnected topics;

- splitting joint chairman and chief executive roles into two distinct, and necessary, jobs;
- ensuring that properly independent non-executive directors are

appointed in sufficient numbers and with sufficient diversity to guarantee that the shareholders' interests are paramount, and that stakeholders' interests are listened to;
- ensuring that members of the board are properly selected and trained to do the policy-formulating and strategic thinking aspects of their work; these are often neglected in the mire of day-to-day management crises.

This last point helps explain the growing internal pressures for board reforms. Recent IOD surveys have shown consistently that over 90 per cent of directors interviewed have had no training or development for their job other than an unstructured accumulated 'experience'. My own work shows that such experience is usually of a managerial, rather than of a directoral, type. Moreover, it shows that the vast majority of directors never really make the move from the operational role of managing to the strategic role of directing. This leaves either one or two very powerful people to drive the business, or, if no one directs it, it creates a black hole in the corporate governance framework at that point where the business brain should be. As external regulatory, economic, and social changes bear down on directors, and as their own personal liabilities grow, there is developing a fast-growing interest in what 'directing' actually is. The awareness that it must be more than just a job title for long-service in managment is beginning to dawn. Demand is now rising for education and development for directors. The UK government's Employment Department is even pushing for certified levels of competence for directors.

What should be clear from this contextual description of the current corporate governance issues in the UK is that although governance *structures* may be readily available to East European economies as models for their own development, the governance *processes* that these structures accommodate still leave a lot to be desired. Post-communist economies have tended to focus on the structural aspects of governance since the challenge, as they see it, is to replace a single state governance structure, which rendered the concept of autonomous corporate governance essentially superfluous, with a multitude of structures competitively embedded in a market process. The message coming out of the UK, the US, Japan, and Western Europe is that process matters too and is ignored at one's peril. The pressure is on from many sources to amend and improve the process and that means the way that directors accomplish their tasks. Existing governance structures may or may not be changed as a result. Process, then, matters, and should not be neglected in discussions of socialist enterprise reform.

GROWING RESPONSES FROM BOARDS

As a consequence of these many pressures, there is a range of different responses from organizations. There is a ready acknowledgement, especially among small and medium sized companies, that 'the board' has often only been a legal formality rather than the locus of direction-giving for the business. If it performed a function at all, it was to provide a setting for a gladitorial contest between power-players in the business rather than offering a forum for reflection and debate amongst equals about a suitable choice of policies and strategies. Making available the time necessary for the central board role to become the 'business brain' – working as a team concentrating on the future of the business and organizing the present resources to achieve that – is a novel concept for 95 per cent of the boards that I have surveyed. Once learned, this role becomes fundamental to designing the future so that it does not end up designing you.

Boards which spend their time looking upwards and outwards are more likely to spot trends and market changes, and be able to respond to them, thus learning to become effective. On the other hand, boards which spend their time looking inwards and downwards may thereby become more efficient but often only at the expense of future corporate effectiveness. In any business, significant profits often come from customers paying premium prices for their perception of your effectiveness, rather than solely compensating you for your internal efficiency – although of course they do this too. It seems wise, therefore, for a board to concentrate on business effectiveness in relation to a fast-changing world as well as on efficiency matters. Overconcentrating on cost-cutting, for example, can often annoy and drive away previously loyal customers. It becomes the managers' job to worry about efficiency once the directors have established the boundaries within which corporate effectiveness will be sought.

If we consider that in socialist enterprises operating in command economies, effectiveness was taken care of by the plan and hence by bureaucrats located outside the enterprise itself – the sole responsibility of enterprise managers was to focus on the efficiency with which the firm's responsibilities under the plan were carried out – it becomes clear that the directing function must constitute a net *addition* to the attributes of the post-communist firm and not merely a rearrangement of the existing internal processes as is commonly supposed by western advisers and consultants.

In their defence, many directors, both east and west, will argue that they have to keep a tight rein over their business or it will fly apart. They already give the majority of their waking time to it and their family and recreational life suffers in consequence. Why should they now do even more? The obvious counter-argument is not for even more work for the overstressed director but for a different, less action-fixated managment style and for more thoughtful action-learning directing.

The current situation is not all doom and gloom despite the additional cost of personal indemnity insurance and the pressure for Chartered Directors. There are signs in the UK, for example, that the need to redefine and re-learn the role of director is being taken very seriously. The IOD report on *Professional Development of and for the Board*, having shown that over 90 per cent of respondents had no training or development for their role, led to the creation of the IOD Centre for Director Development. The number of directors applying for what is believed to be the world's first such centre is gratifyingly large. But there is still a majority of directors which remains puzzled and resentful that the growing public criticism of directors and of their role does not acknowledge their success in creating and maintaining their companies and, by implication, their contribution to the common wealth. There is also real annoyance that the sacrifices they have made through their unbalanced lives, through focusing on their duties to the detriment of family, recreation, and personal health, have gone unappreciated. Do we not hear echoes of this position by the directors of state-owned enterprises in socialist and post-socialist societies?

CREATING A LEARNING BOARD

What can be done to improve matters at the personal, corporate, and public levels? And can it serve as a template for enterprise reformers in post-communist economies? A truly radical approach is needed to cope with the range of pressures currently bearing down on directors of western enterprises. Those with whom I have worked, both on the IOD courses that I run and within companies, typically have had no induction training to the board as a 'top team'. There were no public 'rites of passage' from the managing to the directing in their organization. New directors tend, therefore, to be unsure of their role and of the competences needed to exercise it. It is only now that their lack of basic knowledge of the directing function is being acknowledged and that serious work is being undertaken to rectify it.

Even now the board's responsibilities for giving direction to the business, as distinct from its legal obligations, are not widely known by directors.

The work of Bob Tricker on 'corporate governance' is helpful here as it addresses what is needed to operate effectively behind the boardroom door. His basic model is an essential component of the recently published *Director's Manual*. It outlines four key functions of the board (see Figure 1.1):

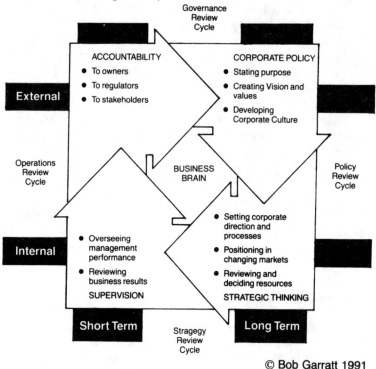

Figure 1.1　Learning cycles of a board

1 Formulating corporate policy
2 Developing strategic thinking
3 Supervising business performance
4 Accounting to owners, etc.

Because of their managerial background, directors naturally see
their main role as directly supervising business performance – a
perception which quickly reverts to directly managing the business
unless it is held in check. There is also a grudging acceptance of
the need to be accountable to the owners. Both of these orientations,
however, are essentially inward–looking and fixated on internal
mechanisms and efficiencies. A more extrovert stance, looking
outward and upwards towards customers and markets, and towards
the world of politics, and of social, economic, technological, and
environmental change, is often treated at best with mild interest
and at worst with derision. Yet, it is in fact the director's outward-
looking orientation that is in most urgent need of development in
Eastern Europe today. I am old-fashioned enough to think that the
title 'director' means that the holder gives direction to his business.
You cannot give direction if you are head down, managing it day-
to-day and hour-to-hour. Giving direction needs a different set of
attitudes, knowledge, and skills from managing. It is this which
the investment managers, professional institutes, and governments
are hinting at with their proposals for professionalizing boards. The
necessary competences are not in themselves hard to acquire –
provided one creates the time necessary to do so and acknowledges
that one is about to re-educate oneself at a time in life when most
people think of education as something behind them. My point is
that it is not ex-socialist managers alone who need to embark
on such learning. Those in market economies on their way to
becoming directors need to do so as well.

To create time means delegating to one's managers and staff the
operational side of the business. It is they who are paid to achieve
results within the framework created by directors. This framework
is fundamental to the continuity and growth of the company. It is
the director's role to supervise what the managers and staff do, but
not to do it for them, even in a small business. Developing the
requisite orientation in effect means creating a 'self-development
contract' for each director. Such a contract is made between the
director himself and either the firm's chairman or its managing
director. It spells out both the developmental needs of each director
and the time and money budgets available to that individual to

meet such needs in the next twelve months. The contract is usually expressed in terms of desirable business results, although some may also emphasize an adequate level of self-development. It is the chairman's job above all to ensure that the board is developing itself to direct. Only then can it begin to flesh out the four key roles mentioned above.

I will go into them in more detail but before I do so, I must acknowledge that I have amended Bob Tricker's quadrant to bring about more of a flow of learning around the board (see Figure 1.1). In so doing I have transposed his strategy and policy aspects so that 'policy' is brought back to its Greek meaning of coping with the political world. In what follows and where appropriate, I shall briefly refer to the applicability of Bob Tricker's model to post-socialist enterprises.

FORMULATING CORPORATE POLICY

Figure 1.1 gives an overview of the board's different tasks set within the directing and regulatory structures of current UK practice. To give effective direction one needs to ensure that the flow of board and organizational learning is rooted firmly in that often neglected, but necessary process, the formulation of corporate policy. The difficulties seen here are often more imagined than real but a vivid imagination can be sufficient to put off a surprising number of directors. Formulating policy, and here I depart from Bob Tricker's model, is about defining the fundamentals of the business, that is:

- stating the purpose of the business;
- creating vision and values that express that purpose;
- developing a corporate culture that serves that purpose.

These are often seen as 'soft' areas which real businesses do not need to take seriously, especially in a recession. However, recession or not, a quick review of the continuing success stories of the industrial world reveals that they are all firmly rooted in well-thought-through and tested policies – that position the total corporation in relation to changing world trends. Policies cannot easily translate into particular figures on the bottom line; but they create the conditions that ensure that there will continue to be a bottom line. Policies may at times seem altruistic or even fuzzy, yet they work because they create the bigger picture – the 'vision'

– to which everyone can subscribe and around which the organization will cohere, and they make manifest to all employees, shareholders, and stakeholders, the values through which business will be done or service provided. Body Shop's values of providing naturalness, and good value for money, through selling environmentally friendly, non-exploitative products to its customers has paid off handsomely over the last decade with comparatively little concentration on the bottom line and a great deal more on the changing world, its customers, and their values. Values can then be internalized by the business as consistent behaviours by all staff from top to bottom. These values and behaviours create the culture – 'the way we do things around here' – that forms the powerful but invisible bonds which develop or destroy the organization. As such, these aspects of policy-formulation are, as some would argue, the critical role of directors. Everything organizational flows from policy formulation.

The formulation of corporate policy will perhaps be the most difficult aspect of corporate governance to grasp fully in post-socialist enterprises. It is easy to see why. In a command economy, the purpose of the business was a 'given' since it was set by the state and by the plan; creating vision and values and a corporate culture to match was never considered to be a *corporate* responsibility but a *political* one. The enterprise was but a channel through which a state-wide ideology was transmitted. The idea that a firm might autonomously develop its own vision and values, under a communist regime, could only be taken as subversive of a higher social purpose. The main danger facing such enterprises today is that the formulation of corporate policy will be greeted by the workforce with the same cynicism as was state policy in its day, '*they* are manipulating *us* once more, so nothing has changed'.

STRATEGIC THINKING

The policies move the learning cycle of the board forward to set the context in which strategic thinking occurs. If policies are about where we are going and why, strategies are about the broad deployment of resources to get there and to ensure that we are effective, and still in tune with the markets, when we arrive.

This second part of the board's cycle of learning is often rushed and can become confused with planning. 'Strategic planning' is an oxymoron, rather like 'friendly fire'. The processes of strategic thinking – of getting into your personal or Board 'helicopter' in order to rise above the day-to-day issues and look at the broader horizon and business-influencing trends – is a learnable and intellectual skill. Directing is an intellectual and reflective process rather than an operational one. It requires much more thought than action.

This is one of the reasons why many managers find becoming a director so difficult. They have invested some twenty to thirty years of their working life in developing a capacity for managerial action, often becoming action-fixated in the process. They find it highly intimidating suddenly to be given the time to think, to observe, and to reflect, and to be told that these are legitimate and necessary directoral activities. They are more used to being energized by the phone ringing with news of an operational crisis, and tend to prefer the immediate problem to the future one.

Yet even abstract and remote intellectual processes have hard edges. The harder edged aspects of strategic thinking include, for example, the thoughtful positioning of the business so as to achieve an optimum impact on its changing markets. It requires that a significant amount of time be put aside by directors to design and regularly monitor the broad changes taking place in the external environment. At a minimum, the use of such techniques as PPEST trend analyses (Physical, Political, Economic, Social, and Technological trends), linked to SWOT analyses (Strengths, Weaknesses, Opportunities, and Threats), and Porter's 'Five Forces' analyses (threats of new entrants, threat of product or service substitution, the economic power of suppliers, and of customers, and the jockeying for position among existing players) become useful for triggering off the strategic thinking processes.

These must be crucially complemented by the board statement on the choice of a corporate orientation that reflects the purpose, vision, and values of the firm, and thus initiates a debate on the strategic deployment of resources. How the basic resources of people, money, physical property, intellectual property, experience, research and development are allocated to achieve both the short-term and long-term business ends must be carefully decided. Many directors find this an uncomfortable process as they resent the time needed to do it well, are often unskilled at doing it at all, and as action-fixated ex-managers, they find the lack of rapid results frustrating. Yet strategic thinking remains a key component of the director's role.

In fostering an organization's learning processes, it is ultimately the ability of directors to become competent at regular and rigorous strategic thought which sorts out the sheep from the goats. It is therefore worth facing the issue at the outset that there is usually no time nor money earmarked for the development of this crucial skill at board level. There is still a deeply held belief that directors are born and not made and therefore, do not need developing or a development budget. Nevertheless some enlightened businesses are now experimenting with the idea of a 'Personal Development Contract' for their directors, budgeting a minimum of ten days per director per year in time and cash and splitting this time budget between personal development activities and board development processes.

The implementation of personal and board development activities faces an even bigger obstacle in Eastern Europe and in the ex-Soviet Union than they do in the West. It is not just that PPEST and SWOT as we have seen were judged irrelevant in a command economy. It is that the associated conception of the firm as a machine that runs on rails at a speed and to a timetable set by the state dispenses with the need for strategic thinking altogether. This is why communist societies inevitably equated the manager with a production engineer. He never had to decide anything, merely to compute it. Uncertainty and risk and the need to adapt one's actions to the vagaries of an uncertain and inhospitable external environment did not register at the level of the socialist enterprise. They were shunted upwards and then dissipated within the labyrinths of the state bureaucracy.

SUPERVISION

At some point, the helicopter where strategic thinking takes place has to come down to earth and confront the realities of day-to-day issues. This is where Supervision comes in because it is where directing touches base with managing and the whole operational cycle of the organization.

Supervision is both the easiest and most difficult of directing tasks. The ease comes through the prior familiarity of many if not most directors with the operations side of the business built up over many years by being part of it. The difficulty, and it is a major one, is in being able to raise operational issues to a level where one can view them critically without immediately wanting to get one's hands on the problems involved and to solve them oneself. Managers and staff are paid to do that. The directors are paid to supervise – to oversee managerial performance without having to prove that they can do better themselves. Not that they would always find this easy. For they need to be able to integrate all of the managerial functions in their thinking. Their dilema then becomes obvious. Most managers have come up through a single functional route to the board. They have been production managers, accountants, lawyers, marketeers, or personnel specialists. So they are often intimidated by the need to ask discriminating questions of other functions than their own since they might look foolish if they do not understand the answer given. The higher-level thinking and learning needed to overcome such bashfulness comes from a director development process which allows each director to look across all business functions and to be comfortable in asking about both the business results of the whole, and each of the parts, without fear of feeling embarrassed or of being fooled by 'techno-babble' from the functinal heads.

Two distinct issues are thus raised concerning the supervising of operations. On the one hand, there is the learnable but often undeveloped skill of asking discriminating questions in areas about which one knows little. This is a directoral skill which can also be described as 'not being conned by expert's jargon'. Obfuscating jargonizing is a well-known technique, employed by many more people than Data Processing managers, when seeking to avoid answering questions. The hope is that the questioner will be so impressed or intimidated by the answer that he will go away before asking more searching questions – I am currently working on the idea of defining the six discriminating questions which can be asked of each specialist function and from which the overall business performance can be determined on a regular and rigorous basis.

With the growth in information technology, it is now technically possible for a board to have at its disposal real-time information systems which will allow it to ask discriminating questions both of its managers and through its integrated IT system. Such technical developments raise intriguing issues concerning the likely behaviour of boards in the twenty-first century, as, for example, whether they need be full-time. Whatever the answer given to this particular question, the key directoral task on this part of the board's learning cycle will continue to be the review of business results. It involves learning how to interrogate a mass of data available weekly, monthly, quarterly, and annually and transforming it into information which will ensure that the organization is following its policies and its strategies in line with its markets, its shareholders' and its stakeholders' interests.

Directional supervision poses a very special challenge in ex-command economies. The irrationalities of socialist accounting had made effective supervision an almost impossible task in the state-owned firm. Supervising bureaux were flooded with a mass of data much of it of dubious accuracy and most of it impossible to interpret. In a post-communist system, effective supervision will be predicated above all on the ready availability to directors of credible and accurate accounting data and on the director's skills in making sense of them. The support potentially available through information technology in such a system must, therefore, await the creation of a viable accounting system that can link the board to the enterprise and the training of enterprise directors in the ways of western accounting concepts.

ACCOUNTABILITY

It is the protection of shareholder and stakeholder interests that complete the board's learning cycle. It is held accountable to them for its leadership of the business. This part of the cycle is the main feedback loop from the firm to the outside world – to owners, regulators, and stakeholders.

The board's accountability to shareholders in the UK is well established in the Companies Acts and Insolvency Act. As I have mentioned these before, I will not repeat myself except to say that further teeth have been added to this legislation, and will continue to be added – probably from outside, as the European Community expands. The issue of personal liability and the profound implications it holds for board members will transform the selection and development of directors over the next decade.

Accountability to regulators is also of growing concern to directors and, again, will form a major theme of the next decade. It is a paradox that as international political strategies focus on improving wealth through the creation of 'level playing fields' both nationally and internationally – the deregulation process – so more regulation appears to define the boundaries of those fields. This has proved so for the Stock Exchange, for banks, and for insurance firms, and it will be so for airlines and for many other industries as we move into the post-1993 European Community. Companies which cross national boundaries will also find that they are increasingly subject to transnational regulators, either worldwide such as GATT, or trading bloc-based such as the North America Free Trade Association or the EC Commission. So at all levels, industrial, national, trading bloc, and global, regulators will be increasingly scrutinizing the actions and the decisions of directors. External scrutiny should concentrate their minds and push them to make sure that they budget sufficiently enough to understand what is happening – and likely to happen – to the regulatory framework within which their firm operates, and to develop their own contribution so that they can make best use of information they receive in giving direction to their organization.

Perhaps the biggest challenge of the twenty-first century for directors, however, will be to take seriously, and respond constructively to, their growing accountability to 'stakeholders'. Drawing on the Porter 'Five Forces' Model, I have already referred to the need to monitor the pressures brought to bear on the firm by customers and suppliers. These are two major stakeholders in the business but they are not the only ones. To them needs be added the staff, who have deep personal investment in the organization, and the wider community. This 'community' notion is at present still fuzzy but there are now some discernible hard edges to it. The request for planning permission to develop or redevelop a site belonging to a firm, for example, usually gives a sharp insight into the varied and contradictory pressures which run in a community – from local employment, to the effect on house and industrial building prices, through to the disruption of community values, to green challenges with possibly national or even international implications. These raise both business and ethical issues which need serious board discussion. In turn, they lead us back once more into the area of corporate policy as we recheck our Purpose, Vision, Values, and Culture and carry out necessary adjustments. The wheel thus comes full circle.

Accountability as described here will be an entirely new concept for post-communist directors. For along with it not only have their responsibilities now been expanded to accommodate policy formulation, strategic thinking, and credible supervision, but in parallel so has the constituency to whom they are accountable. In a command economy one stakeholder predominated: the state. It eclipsed all others. Managers and directors were not required to arbitrate and balance out competing claims and to that extent their discretionary power was much reduced. Meeting the expectations of the state meant carrying out state orders, not interpreting and mitigating them. Accountability in Eastern Europe will only fully come into play as a governance issue when institutional structures exist to empower various stakeholder groups linked to them, and to transmit their expectations to the board of directors.

CONCLUSION

I hope that I have given sufficient indications of the way that the director's job will develop in the near future. It is both different from managing, and requires a considerable investment in time, in its own right, if it is to impart a sense of direction to a business. The boards that I see developing well in this area tend to have a regular cycle of board meetings which are anything but formal. They are energetic and constructively critical sessions of strategic thinking, exchange of ideas, debate, and direction-giving which lead the business forward. A typical round might start with an annual Policy Review Cycle which would set the scene for at least half-yearly Strategy Review Cycles. In turn, these might provide the framework for at least monthly Operations Review Cycles, the results of which would feed back into an annual Governance Cycle. The latter would raise questions to be addressed at the next annual policy review.

Such a rolling process is designed to turn what are often vicious circles of non-learning by a board into virtuous learning cycles, in which directors can gradually come to understand their roles, the values of their business, the policies and strategies they need to create for a sustainable production of wealth.

Where might such developments in the director's role leave enterprises in a reforming Eastern Europe or ex-Soviet Union? The state-owned firm of the command economy and the joint-stock firm of the market economy share one characteristic that is common to all forms of hierarchical organization: the top is primarily concerned with problems of effectiveness and the base with problems of efficiency. The main difference is that in the command economy, the top is located outside the firm and embedded in the state structure whereas in the market economy it is institutionalized as the board of directors. If western firms have problems in shifting managers away from concerns with efficiency and towards issues of effectiveness as they move up to board level, how much more is this going to be true of the managers of state-owned enterprises who have no experience of effectiveness issues at the enterprise level at all.

In post-communist societies, therefore, changes that are currently sought in management practices will be largely wasted if they are not carried out in harmony with changes in the governance processes that will make them effective. The creation of western type governance structures, as experience in the UK and elsewhere amply attests, of itself, will not suffice. It is what goes on within the structure that will count. The learning cycle, I believe, with its emphasis on process, points the way forward.

DISCUSSION OF BOB GARRATT'S PRESENTATION

Jane Salk asked who should properly be considered a director in Bob Garratt's scheme. Should it only be outsiders or should top management also qualify? Bob Garratt replied that a director is a person who gives direction to an organization and he sees that as being quite different from managing it. Top management might therefore qualify, but only under certain quite restrictive conditions.

Lee Vansina warned that in an international setting, the term director has different meanings for different people. In Eastern Europe or in China , for example, the term is confined to the senior executives of the enterprise. External directors are unheard of. The functions of the director are, therefore, quite different and it becomes important to spell out specifically what competences a director in the western sense of the term is required to have.

Imre Spronz commented that even within the context of the socialist enterprise, as a general manager he found himself caught between competing claims by different stakeholders. Because many of these could be said to equally represent the owners – i.e. commissions, bureaux, central ministries – there is little institutional guidance on how to deal with them. He felt that the West's experience of *directing*, in Bob Garratt's sense of the term, would not be easily transferable without massive institutional changes in the governance structure of firms and the legal framework of property rights.

Bob Garratt replied that such governance issues are far from being resolved in the West and that the institutional changes currently taking place in Eastern Europe might well provide learning opportunities for both sides.

Tom Lupton pointed out that competent direction requires competent directors, people with an ability to develp a firm. Identifying and developing such people will remain a major challenge in Eastern Europe for years to come for they are not necessarily well placed to be promoted at present.

Jan-Peter Paul believed that the problem of direction in the West is compounded by the short time horizons held by major stake-holders – the bank lending to the firm, workers in quest of an immediate pay rise, shareholding pension funds looking for steady dividends, etc. Given the urgency of the problem in Eastern Europe, the pressure for short-term performance exerted on direc-tors could only get worse. As a result, directors in ex-socialist economies are constantly neglecting policy and strategic issues in order to concentrate on firefighting at the operational level. From being directors, in effect, they either become *de facto* managers or, worse, management second-guessers. Sportis, as so many other small firms in the region, provides ample evidence of such behaviour.

Max Boisot, summarizing, felt that the problems of directing in Eastern Europe would be compounded in foreign joint ventures. In the case of western firms, governance structures are firm-specific and autonomous. In Eastern Europe, they link the firm to the state administration. Remove that administration and the logic behind the existing governance process disappears. East European managers are simply not used to the freedom and responsibilities that accompany autonomous corporate governance (for evidence of this, see the presentation by John Child and Livia Markoczy, Chapter 7).

Chapter 2

The lessons from China

Max Boisot

INTRODUCTION

During the 1980s the centre of gravity of US trade shifted from the Atlantic to the Pacific, reflecting both the increasing interdependence of the North American and the Japanese economies and the emergence of newly industrializing Asian countries as participants in world trade. China was prominent among these. Having made a few cautious moves towards some form of market economy in the agricultural sector, the country appeared to be launched on a set of economic reforms that appeared wellnigh irreversible (Warner 1987; Tidrick and Jiyuan Chen 1987).

None of these developments appeared to augur well for Europe. The old continent, it was said, exhausted by two world wars, plagued by economic fragmentation, and paralyzed by fractious nation states, was suffering from a disease labelled 'Eurosclerosis'. Would history now pass it by on its way to the dynamic shores of the Pacific?

History, of course, rarely gives definite answers to questions such as these. It merely offers hints and leaves us to make what we can of these. Here, then, are three such hints that might encourage a new kind of speculation concerning Europe's future.

1 The Tianamen Square massacre of June 1989 threw the Chinese economic reforms into reverse for three years. Foreign investment, consequently, mostly ground to a halt and Hong Kong's prospects, under an imminent reassertion of Chinese sovereignty, took a nose dive. There is new movement on the reform front, but for how long? The Chinese commitment to economic reform, official proclamations notwithstanding, remains fragile.

2 The Single European Act has given the old continent a new

impetus towards market integration and a new vision of itself. Was Eurosclerosis, therefore, a genuine ailment or just a bout of hypochondria?

3 The 1989 revolution in Eastern Europe has created a 'new frontier' within Europe itself that might get considerably extended in an eastward direction in a foreseeable future if it incorporates the most viable remnants of the now disintegrated Soviet Empire. Could Europe also become a Pacific power, as Russia has already claimed to be, if the latter is brought into its orbit?

The kaleidoscopic changes of 1989 and 1991 will not of themselves scotch talk of the 'Pacific century'. Asian growth rates may be maintained, the old men in Beijing may finally fade away, democratizing Eastern Europe could yet stumble. Yet they do caution against a facile historical determinism. A resurgent Europe whose growth was fuelled by a mix of market reforms – market integration with the EC itself, and a move towards a market order in Eastern Europe and the ex-USSR – would pose a formidable challenge to the recently established conventional wisdom that the Asia-Pacific region is set to dominate the world economy in the twenty-first century.

The move away from communism in Eastern Europe is unlikely to follow the Chinese path; the problems and the opportunities are too different. When China embarked on its reform programme in 1979, the country was virtually free of debt; it was 'under-borrowed' as a credit-happy banker might put it. The countries of Eastern Europe, by contrast, were heavily indebted. Yet Eastern Europe is likely to enjoy a level of institutional and economic support from industrialized countries that was simply unavailable to China from 1979 to 1989. There are two basic reasons for this. The first is that these countries are not seeking reform within a communist framework but rather seeking to do away with the framework altogether, so that political reform presently ranks at least as high on the agenda as economic reform. The second is that the reform process is being initiated from a far higher level of social and economic development, and in the context of cultures and traditions that are essentially European – i.e. Judeo-Christian – rather than Confucian (Pye 1985).

Do these differences mean that the Chinese experience of a market order, limited as it was, has no relevance for western firms wishing to invest in Eastern Europe? Were the circumstances that confronted Volkswagen in Shanghai or Otis Elevators in Tianjin specific to China's culture and traditions, or are we likely to see a replay of some of the challenges they had to contend with?

As was the case with the PRC, the joint venture has been mooted as one of the major vehicles of collaboration between foreign and domestic firms in Eastern Europe and in the USSR. In China, however, the joint venture only gained official acceptance when it became clear that the country lacked the foreign exchange to pay for needed inputs. The offshore oil that was to have secured the necessary foreign exchange earning never really materialized, and therefore the arm's length importation of western technology that the Chinese leadership had originally sought ceased to be a viable option.

Joint ventures, therefore, came to be perceived as transferring a sophisticated bundle of needed inputs which the country lacked the sophistication to acquire and use in an unbundled form. Prior to Tianamen Square, the country had built up seven to eight years of experience with Sino-foreign joint ventures, most of it very mixed, and much of it wholly negative.

This paper sets out to interpret that experience in the light of China's reform policies and to tease out of it potentially important lessons for would-be foreign investors in Eastern Europe. In the next section we review some of the main characteristics of China's experience of collaboration with foreign investors, going on to briefly present the results of some field research on Sino-foreign joint ventures carried out by the China–EC Management Institute in Beijing in 1988 and 1989. We then look at the reform environment in which these joint ventures took place, identifying similarities and differences with the current situation in Eastern Europe. In the penultimate section a simple conceptual scheme provides a framework for interpreting the Chinese experience and for assessing the prospects of success in Eastern Europe. A concluding section explores the policy implications of our analysis for prospective investors in Eastern Europe.

SINO-FOREIGN COLLABORATION

The open door policy initiated in 1979 had made Chinese leaders acutely aware of just how far the country had fallen behind since 1949 – not just behind industrialized countries such as, say, the UK, which Mao had vowed to overtake economically by the early 1970s but even newly industrialized countries such as the four

Asian Dragons which at mid–century had hardly been thought of as fit candidates for modernization at all.

Backwardness in technology was the most visible symptom of China's problem and it was naturally assumed that catching up in technology would therefore be the most visible symbol of the country's ability to overcome the problem.

Steeped in a tradition of self-reliance, the challenge was to obtain this technology without getting ensnared in a web of dependencies which would tie the country to the West. China had experienced such dependency since the Opium Wars of the mid-nineteenth century and was determined to avoid it.

The policy initially adopted was one of arm's length technology acquisition either through equipment purchasing or through technology licensing agreements. The foreign exchange necessary for purchasing would come from exports, initially from raw materials such as oil – the South China Seas were viewed as promising in this respect – and, as the economy modernized, from buy-back arrangements of products manufactured with the technologies licensed. Thus there would be no need to open up the domestic market to foreign firms and hence to import institutional and cultural as well as technological changes. The old structure was not perfect, everybody knew that, but it was believed that by tinkering a bit with it at the edges, some of its more glaring inefficiencies could be eliminated, and it could be made to serve for a while yet. Cautious incrementalism was the order of the day.

Things did not work out that way. The bounty promised by offshore oil proved elusive and, indeed, still remains so, and the poor quality of Chinese manufactured goods made them unmarketable in the West, whether through barter or direct sale. By 1983 it had become apparent that the country would lack the foreign exchange to dictate the terms on which it would be given access to western and Japanese technology and that, therefore, more intimate forms of involvement with foreigners such as joint ventures would have to be envisaged.

From 1983 onward, the joint venture was officially to become the preferred vehicle for Sino-foreign collaboration. It took two forms:

1 The contractual joint venture was an agreement entered into between a domestic Chinese firm and a foreign firm in which both the task and the remuneration of the foreign partner were both specified and limited. There was little pooling of risks and

rewards and, in western terms, it should be rated closer to a subcontracting arrangement than a joint venture.

2 The equity joint venture (EJV) did involve a pooling of risks and rewards by both parties and actually called for a much greater resource commitment by the foreign investor.

These forms of collaboration were promulgated by the Chinese leadership with scant appreciation of the legal and institutional changes they required, and it was only the very cautious response of the foreign business community that led to an attempt over the next few years to forge a business environment more responsive to the needs of prospective investors (Ruggles 1983). What were the obstacles to foreign investment that the leadership was being urged to attend to?

Perhaps the most important was the absence of any credible legal framework to protect the interests of foreign investors. Laws were indistinguishable from administrative regulations and were often either unwritten or not publicly available in a written form. The concept of the judicial process was almost unknown and a Confucian preference for harmony made litigation a hazardous undertaking for both parties to a dispute.

Next in order of importance came the uncertainty of supply conditions. The arbitrariness and inefficiency of the planning mechanism meant that a joint venture could never be certain when orders would be delivered, whether the quantity delivered would bear any relationship to the quantity ordered, and whether deliveries would match the specifications of the order. The quality of inputs was extremely poor but brave was the manager who would dare to refuse a delivery on that account.

Thirdly came personnel matters. Chinese policy-makers were selling the idea of joint ventures on the basis of low labour costs: the average worker in a Chinese state-owned enterprise was earning about £40 a month. Joint ventures, however, were being asked to pay perhaps twice or sometimes three times these salary figures with the state pocketing the difference. Yet even the higher wage did not itself make labour expensive. What did was its abysmally low productivity and lack of skill. The unit labour cost of a Hitachi Television manufacturing joint venture in Fuzhou, for example, was higher than for an equivalent plant in Japan. Part of the labour problem was institutional: local labour bureaux assigned unnecessarily large contingents of workers to joint ventures and as soon as these were trained, in many cases, they would be reassigned to

Chinese plants. At another level, Chinese authorities, citing the principle of equal pay for equal work, would insist on having the foreign joint venture partner pay the Chinese managers of a joint venture exactly the same salary as his foreign counterpart – in foreign exchange, of course. The Chinese manager himself would actually receive only his usual salary – set at about 40 per cent higher than that of a manual worker. The state, as usual, would pocket the difference.

In general there was an expectation on the Chinese side that foreign investors would adapt their managerial styles to local practices, which then made it difficult to use joint ventures as the learning opportunities they could have been. Their commercial attractiveness was further undermined by a tendency to overcharge them for inputs often made deliberately scarce by the opportunistic behaviour of local officials able to exploit their monopoly of distribution channels.

Many of the problems just cited were in fact exacerbated by the urban economic reforms set in motion in October 1984. A delegation of administrative power first to provincial and then to urban authorities coincided with a decentralization of power from these local authorities to industrial enterprises.

In effect, the first largely nullified the second (Boisot and Child 1988). The much-heralded 'responsibility systems' – the enterprise responsibility system, the contract responsibility system, the director responsibility system, and the variants thereof – were designed to put some distance between local industrial bureaux which reported to local territorial administrations, and industrial enterprises under their care. The latter were to assume direct responsibility for their profits and losses, were to be allowed to sell off-quota production on the open market, and in a general way, were to be allowed managerial discretion in the conduct of enterprise affairs.

Results were mixed. To be sure, enterprise managers, when asked, *felt* themselves to have somewhat more room for manoeuvre than under the old planning dispensation. But when their managerial discretion was placed alongside that of western managers of equivalent official rank, it became quickly apparent that they had little more scope than the first-line supervisor in a western manufacturing plant and that the threads that tied them to their supervisory bureaucracy were as tight as ever (Child and Lu 1989; Boisot and Child 1988; Boisot and Xing 1992).

From the perspective of a foreign investor used to operating under the old regime, a decentralization to local authorities in which the central authorities quickly lost control, meant that instead of sorting out his problems at ministry level once and for all, he now often found himself having to deal with several levels of an administrative hierarchy, each with its own agenda, but now with an ability to 'squeeze' him discreetly for economic rents.

In assessing the implications of such difficulties for would-be investors in Eastern Europe, the challenge is to factor out those features of the situation that might be attributable to what one might loosely term 'cultural variables' and those that might result from the systematic properties of a Marxist-Leninist framework. Yet even if one was able to do this, the reciprocal influence that culture and institutional structure exert on each other over time makes it difficult to view them respectively as autonomous levels of explanation. Forty years of communism has woven a fabric of values and beliefs that can only be called cultural even if it had to build on a base of compatible values and expectations. In a later section we shall try to identify those features of the Chinese reform experience which can be attributed to structural/institutional factors and hence transposable to the East European case, and those which might be properly viewed as belonging to the cultural domain proper. Tentative as such an exercise will be, however, I shall not argue that the cultural problem has no implications for post-communist Eastern Europe. Before doing this, we first present some enterprise-specific data on Sino-foreign collaboration in China.

SINO-FOREIGN JOINT VENTURES: A STUDY

By 1989 Sino-foreign joint ventures have become the Chinese leadership's preferred vehicle for the modernization of Chinese state-owned enterprises from outside. An article published in *The People's Daily* of 3 October 1989 entitled 'Adhere to Opening to the Outside World', claimed that 11,285 equity joint ventures (EJV) had been approved to date and that these represented 55.6 per cent of all foreign direct investment in the PRC. Total contracted investments by EJV stood at US $10.8 billion with US $6.4 billion already committed. Campbell (1988) has urged caution in the use of such figures since other sources cite 2,136 EJV's in operation and US $3.8 billion committed. Campbell also noted that Hong Kong and Macao accounted for 70.6 per cent of total EJV investments and

76.6 per cent of the total number of projects. Those from the US accounted for 9.3 per cent of EJV's by value and 7.9 per cent by number, with Japanese EJV's making up 7.3 per cent of EJV investment value and 7.2 per cent of projects. EC EJV's trailed behind, accounting for 6.8 per cent of investment value and 2.9 per cent of projects.

In this section, drawing on some of the same data as John Child and Livia Markoczy in their presentation (Chapter 7), we briefly describe some field research carried out between 1988 and 1989 on the managerial styles of Sino-foreign joint ventures by the China–EC Management Institute in Beijing (CEMI). Sino-foreign collaboration has been the focus of a certain amount of attention (NCUSCT 1987; Hendryx 1986) in view of the problems experienced by foreign investors in the PRC. Yet, whereas earlier studies had tended to concentrate on broad institutional issues external to the venture, the CEMI study examined the internal managerial processes.

In all, thirty joint ventures were chosen for the study, twenty-three of which were located in Beijing and another seven outside Beijing. It is recognized that conditions can vary considerably from one part of China to another, particularly subsequent to the administrative decentralization that occurred in the 1980s so that the sample studied may contain some bias. Yet the authors of the study do not believe that regional variations would have modified their conclusion. All the joint ventures had been in operation for at least a year and the foreign investment involved ranged from a paltry US $250,000 to over US $200 million. Predictably the numbers employed by the joint venture also varied considerably: from thirty-one people in the smallest to 4,300 in the largest. The national origin of the foreign joint venture partners is given in Table 2.1. Clearly, given the heavy representation of Hong Kong and Macao in EJV's in the PRC, the above sample cannot claim to be statistically representative. It reflects the availabliity of firms for what was intended to be primarily a qualitative piece of research.

A basic theme of this research was the possible relationship that might be found inside the joint venture between formalization and centralization. Studies of organizational structure have indicated that formalization is likely to vary with size and task complexity (Pugh et al. 1969) if everything else is equal. Of interest here was the fact that everything else would not be equal so that cultural and institutional factors might also play a part.

Table 2.1 Profile of sample

National Origin of Number of JV's studied	Foreign JV partner
Europe	11
US	7
Japan	7
Hong Kong	5
TOTAL	30

What, then, might distinguish Sino-foreign EJV's from the mere run-of-the-mill industrial enterprises that the western world is familiar with? And what effect might this have on the venture's managerial style?

Perhaps the most striking *organizational* feature that set these firms apart from western models was their importation of a parallel managerial command structure from Chinese political practice. The typical Chinese state-owned enterprise has a party structure that operates alongside the managerial one with powers of control and interference. In the EJV's the dual structure was not political but in most cases there was a Chinese counterpart for every expatriate and, in effect, very little integration of Chinese and foreign managerial practices. Three firms in the sample were exclusively managed by the chinese side; the remainder were jointly managed and this resulted in problems of coordination as tasks were tackled from radically different perspectives (Killing 1982).

With two exceptions, the management of personnel was the responsibility of the Chinese partner to the venture and production and marketing tended to fall to the foreign partners. Two interpretations are possible. The first holds that China, like Japan, tends to elevate the personnel function to a key position in the firm, the latter for reasons of corporate culture, the former because it is an effective transmission belt both for state sponsored ideology and for state policies. To the extent that the Chinese perceive the value of Sino-foreign collaboration as residing essentially in the technical area – and in the PRC, even western management is still widely perceived to consist essentially of statistical and engineering techniques applied to production processes – they remain concerned to protect the 'soft' areas of the collaboration from domination by foreign ideas and values.

The second interpretation, which complements rather than

excludes the first, is that foreign investors setting up in China encounter a culture that is experienced as opaque, institutional practices of forbidding complexity, and a social and economic environment for which they feel themselves to have little operating competence. By focusing on production and marketing problems they effectively put themselves on neutral territory since these are areas that are considered by their local partners as ones to which they can legitimately contribute.

The above considerations help to explain why most foreign managers interviewed claimed that the EJV's personnel policies were very different to what was practised back in their home country. Some of these differences are easily summarized:

- The practice of democratic centralism had promoted a passive, responsibility-shy, participative style among Chinese managers. They tended to be punished for committing errors rather than rewarded for taking initiatives. The observed result was a reluctance by individuals with managerial promise to accept promotion to positions where they would have responsibilities for others. To complicate matters, promotion of Chinese staff inside an EJV at the request of the foreign partner may have little perceived legitimacy. It may be done to satisfy the foreign partner's requirement for managerial flexibility but it may have little or no official status with either the local personnel or labour bureau. These are located outside the enterprise and in the local authority. In the typical case they powerfully influence the behaviour of enterprises in matters of personnel. Chinese staff whose promotion in the EJV has not been officially 'blessed' by these 'mothers-in-law', as such bureaux are known in China, are likely to play safe and maintain their earlier behaviour patterns, the exhortations of foreign partners notwithstanding.

- The reluctance to accept responsibility goes hand in hand with a strong resistance to salary differentials. Chinese egalitarianism has been viewed as the fruit of forty years of socialization to a communist ideology. Whilst inherited values and beliefs may be important, there are other equally plausible explanations for the intense egalitarianism that prevails in Chinese enterprises. The most obvious perhaps concerns the lack of economic rationality in the system. The command economy diffuses irrationality throughout Chinese industry and particularizes the relationship between firms and their supervising bureaucracy – Kornai's 'soft budget constraint' (Kornai 1986). Poorly performing firms are subsidized and well-performing firms are taxed in such a way that it becomes almost impossible to devise credible and independent measures of performance either at the level of the enterprise as a whole or at that of individuals or departments within the enterprise. To offer individuals differential rewards on the basis of such arbitrary and unreliable performance measures would be a recipe for permanent conflict and resentment. For this reason, for example, bonuses designed to stimulate individual effort and intiative were, for the most part, distributed in equal measure to all, irrespective of performance.

- Chinese industrial firms are considered to be extensions of the state bureaucracy that supervises their operations and hence are channels for the implementation of government policy. Official rhetoric on the need to give Chinese managers more autonomy and measures to achieve this hardly made a dent in this fundamental relationship between the state and the firm. One of the key functions of the industrial firm in China is to redeem, on behalf of the state, the socialist pledge of full employment. In practical terms this means that the managerial discretion to hire and fire is not available to the director of a Chinese firm. EJV's, which on paper enjoyed the right to hire and fire, quickly discovered that in practice this right was almost impossible to exercise without a lengthy haggle with either the supervising bureaucracy or with the Chinese managers of the joint venture. The underlying premise for Chinese managers is that job security is a reward for loyalty rather than performance, and in the PRC, professions of loyalty and devotion are not hard to come by. Foreign joint venture partners found it particularly difficult to persuade the personnel department in their organizations that these were at the service of the firm itself and not of the supervising bureaucracies.

As we shall see, foreign investors varied in how far they were willing to adapt their own managerial practices to the situation described above. US EJV's in the sample turned out to be the most forceful in introducing their style of management in China. They were more likely to have introduced training schemes, to have reformed remuneration systems and, generally, to have adopted formal procedures in their day-to-day administration. For this reason US EJV's mentioned problems of work relationships and behaviour twice as often as European and Japanese ones and four times as frequently as Hong Kong ones. This is consistent with the

Table 2.2 Proportion of EJVs reporting no
formalization procedures

Foreign Partner	Percentage
Japan	71%
Hong Kong	60%
EC	55%
US	29%

data of Table 2.2 which shows US firms to be most prone to the use of formal procedures and Japanese ones the least. Indeed the latter group made little attempt to introduce Japanese management methods in China since they found themselves unable to communicate corporate goals or, more generally, to forge the kind of strong corporate identity on which their managerial style depends.

There are several possible explanations for the comparatively higher degree of formalization found in US EJV's. Firstly, their share of the equity contributed to the venture was higher than for the rest of the sample and, possibly for that reason, they employed a larger number of expatriates. Secondly, they constituted the larger joint ventures in the sample so that their increased formalization could merely be the expression of a size effect. Thirdly, they had a longer contract life than other EJV's so that the stakes involved were perceived to be higher. And finally, they tended to be much more willing transferors of their technology so that their managerial problems, being therefore that much more complex, would be in greater need of formalization.

In spite of these differences, US EJV partners shared with the rest of the sample two striking characteristics. The first was that managerial activities which would normally have been formalized in the home country, were not in China. There was something about the Chinese managerial environment that was refractory to high formalization. The second was that even their higher degree of formalization did not allow decentralization. Chinese managers remained notoriously reluctant to accept any form of responsibility which made any attempt at delegation problematic.

How is one to interpret these features of the Chinese managerial environment? It had been initially assumed by the researchers, given their familiarity with the Chinese economic reforms, that problems external to the enterprise – i.e. of foreign exchange, infrastructure, supplies, the supervisory bureaucracy, changes in government policies, arbitrary administrative regulations, etc. –

would be experienced by foreign investors as the main causes of their headaches. This was not so: the problems most frequently mentioned in interview were *internal* to the joint venture and related to employee attitudes, the lack of motivation, the casual approach to quality, and above all to communications. Why communications? Because in the PRC, access to information is not considered a right but a privilege: only the bureaucratic elite is entitled to it and it conserves it as a source of bureaucratic power. There is no horizontal flow of information of an official kind either within a firm or between firms except through a well-developed grapevine that acts as much to misinform as to inform. Managers therefore obtain the information they need through personal relationships, *guanxi*, an informal network that is built up over time as an aid to individual survival in a highly uncertain environment.

Internal managerial problems, however, are not as divorced from external problems as may appear. Child and Lu (1990) point to the difficulty of achieving managerial autonomy at the enterprise level in China given the absence of codification at the level of local government with respect to key elements such as law and taxation. It is this external uncertainty, imported into the firm, that makes it so hard to set up formal managerial procedures on a solid footing. External agencies – the 'mothers-in-law' – are constantly interfering with enterprise business for their own purposes, destabilizing managerial practices and robbing managers of whatever authority they might possess. This proved to be as major a source of difficulties for EJVs in China as for indigenous firms and goes a long way towards explaining the inability to formalize organizational procedures and hence to decentralize them.

CHINA AND EASTERN EUROPE – SIMILARITIES AND DIFFERENCES

Eastern Europe is not China. Prior to 1949, China was a country of appalling misery as well as poverty, having only just emerged from a brutal civil war and an even more brutal occupation by the Japanese. Its industrialization, modest as it was, had been limited to a few cities along the coast and one or two urban centres along the Yangtze such as Nanjing and Wuhan. China's culture was that of a rural and backward economy shot through with an exploitative feudalism and great inequalities of power and wealth. In such a country, providing that people's eyes could be kept focused on the nation's recent past rather than on how neighbours were progressing, the advent of communism could plausibly be experienced as a 'liberation' – indeed this is the term still used when referring to 1949 – rather than an enthralment, a step towards utopia that would eliminate insecurity and starvation.

Not so in Eastern Europe, parts of which before the war had enjoyed one of the highest levels of industrialization in the western world. Here communism was experienced as the imposition of a retrograde order by an alien and backward culture set on world domination.

Does the difference of circumstances in which communist ideology was encountered not explain differences in local attitudes towards social evolution and reform? In Eastern Europe, freeing oneself from the shackles of foreign domination meant shaking off the ideology through which that domination was imposed and returning to forms of social and economic organization that had earlier enjoyed considerable success and that were expressive of Europe's long-term cultural evolution.

In China, by contrast, in spite of a strong consensus that reform was needed, communism was viewed with much more ambivalence. Following the open door policy, a generation that had grown up free of the hunger and deprivation of the 1920s and 1930s became suddenly much more aware than its elders of the country's failure to modernize and keep up with its neighbours. The older generation felt differently, and whilst willing to tinker with the economic machinery of Marxist-Leninism in order to speed up the pace of modernization, it was not willing to write off a system which was still viewed by many as progressive and capable of further improvement.

These considerations explain two features of the Chinese reforms that distinguish them from those envisaged in Eastern Europe. Firstly, they are oriented to a far greater extent than western observers realize towards the finding of a middle way between a socialist and a capitalist economic order – indeed, most reform measures initiated since 1978 owe far more to the failed Hungarian model of market socialism of the late 1960s (Kornai 1986) or to Lenin's New Economic Policies (NEP) of 1921–8 than to any western model, official Chinese rhetoric to the contrary notwithstanding. In this way the new order can be presented as a natural evolution of the old one, faces are saved, and both communism and its leadership survive.

Secondly, any conflict that surfaces as a result of the reform process – or of its failure, given its tendency to fall between two stools – will be experienced as a conflict between generations, between those who participated in the 'long march' and those who settled for a 'walkman'.

A Confucian concern to preserve social harmony between contending groups led the Chinese leaders to avoid making hard choices between markets and hierarchies; they would have a little bit of both and if in doing so they could not please everyone, at least nobody would be outraged. By 1988 the result was fairly widespread chaos and corruption as the internal logic of what should have been competing alternatives was gradually eroded by an impossible and quite artificial coexistence between them.

The Chinese reform failure can be interpreted in two ways, not necessarily exclusive. The first, and perhaps the most popular in the western press, points to a failure of courage by the Chinese leadership fully to grasp the reform nettle and to take the consequences. Although I do not discard such an interpretation – I believe that it explains a good deal – I believe that a more important failure was one of understanding. By their policies and their behaviour, the Chinese leaders indicated that not only had they little or no idea of what a market order amounted to, but perhaps more seriously, they also revealed serious gaps in their grasp of socialism and its Marxist variants. Had that understanding been present, perhaps there would have been something to be courageous about.

In other words, what I am asserting here is that the Chinese failure to move towards a market order may be predicated in part on a failure first to build up a viable bureaucratic base, albeit a Marxist-Leninist one, essential to the efficient functioning of market processes. Whereas European capitalism was built upon the solid rational-legal foundations of the absolutist state, in China the bureaucracy remained stubbornly patrimonial and expressive of an earlier feudal order, and this even *after* the advent of communism (Boisot and Child 1988).

Would such an interpretation render the Chinese experience of reform inapplicable in Eastern Europe? Will the social and economic environment experienced by foreign investors be completely different in each case? The issue needs careful consideration.

Both Eastern Europe and China experienced the Soviet model of economic organization, the former as imposed from above, the latter as indiscriminate borrowing. Thus in both regions one will encounter State Planning and Economic Commissions, industrial bureaux, 'soft budget constraints' and 'investment hunger' (Kornai, 1986). The problems internal to industrial enterprises in Eastern Europe that were identified by Granik (1987) in many instances bear a striking similarity to those uncovered in Chinese firms by Boisot and Child (1988) and by Child and Lu (1990).

Yet the Soviet model in the first case was grafted on to a highly developed industrial structure which it slowed down but did not destroy, and in the second case was attached to an undeveloped feudal structure which, partly as a result, was unable to grow a rational-legal bureaucratic order. Both Eastern Europe and China suffered a loss of economic rationality as a result of their encounter with Marxist-Leninism but with very different consequences. We explore this in the next section by means of a simple conceptual model.

A CONCEPTUAL MODEL

Western critics of command economies have attacked them on two grounds: they are wanting in rationality – the all-seeing bureaucrat who efficiently allocates myriad resources instead of leaving it to the market does not exist – and they concentrate power. In fact, the two problems are intimately related: only decisions that have some coherence and rationality can in fact be formalized and then decentralized.

This relationship between decentralization and formalization is depicted in Figure 2.1. It is implicit in many of the organization studies carried out by the Aston Research Group in the 1960s and 1970s (Pugh *et al.* 1969) and has been further elaborated from an information perspective by Boisot (1986, 1987). The diagram depicts a decision environment from which emerges a simple typology of institutional arrangements. These can be found in · various combinations inside as well as outside firms and other organizational forms. The typology is described in more detail in Figure 2.2.

It should be stressed that the term formalization, as it is used here, goes beyond the mere act of setting things down on paper and filling out pre-printed forms. It captures the rationality dimension in its ability to simplify, to reduce complex issues to simple choices. Thus, for example, for us the extreme of formalization is

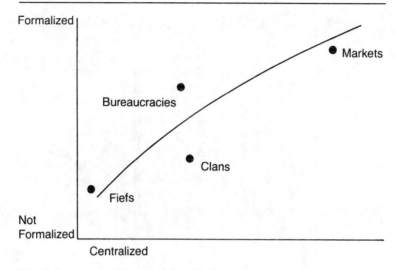

Figure 2.1   Decentralization and formalization

achieved by the concept of a market price, in which the multiple determinants of economic value are codified in a single monetary measure. It is precisely because a market price represents an extreme of formalization that it becomes the appropriate vehicle for achieving an extreme of decentralization – the market – in which hierarchical coordination has all but been abolished. Conversely, when the information that goes into decisions is not even talked about, let alone put down on paper – whether because such information is ineffable or because its possessor wishes to hold on to it – it ceases to be available for the purposes of coordination beyond the information source itself. No decentralization is then possible, and the power that acccrues to the decision centre is entirely personal. Hence the label 'fief' to describe this region of the space. The remaining institutional forms, bureaucracies and clans, are self explanatory.

Students of culture have noted that the degree to which decisions are formalized can be culture-specific (Hall 1977; Hofstede 1980; Boisot 1986). Some have explicitly linked formalization to social and economic evolution (Tonnies 1887; Durkheim 1933) thus suggesting some kind of trajectory over time up the diagonal of Figure 2.2. Strong versions of this view go by the name of the convergence hypothesis: industrialization pushes towards homogeneous forms of organization and gradually robs cultures of their

	Centralized	Decentralized
Formalized	**2 Bureaucracies** • Information diffusion limited and under central control • Relationships impersonal and hierarchical • Submission to superordinate goals • Hierarchical coordination • No necessity to share values and beliefs	**3 Markets** • Information widely diffused, no control • Relationships impersonal and competitive • No superordinate goals – each one for himself • Horizontal coordination through self-regulation • No necessity to share values and beliefs
Not formalized	**1 Fiefs** • Information diffusion limited by lack of codification to face-to-face relationships • Relationships personal and hierarchical (feudal/charismatic) • Submission to superordinate goals • Hierarchical coordination • Necessity to share values and beliefs	**4 Clans** • Information is diffused but still limited by lack of codification to face-to-face relationships • Relationships personal but nonhierarchical • Goals are shared through a process of negotiation • Horizontal coordination through negotiation • Necessity to share values and beliefs

Figure 2.2 A typology of institutional arrangements

specificity (Galbraith 1967; Rostow 1960). The hypothesis remains controversial and for this reason what follows is not intended to address the issues it raises, much as it may be considered relevant.

The research presented above points to a very strong bias towards informal face-to-face relationships in Chinese organizations. This view is supported by investigations into the institutional environment of the Chinese economic reforms (Boisot and Child 1988). The observed centralization in the joint venture sample is consistent with this lack of formalization and it indirectly supports the research findings on the lack of formalization itself.

At first sight, the phenomenon is surprising. Many westerners, on arrival in China, encounter a massive bureaucracy – China Inc. – the supreme expression of Marxist-Leninist ideology. Yet appearances are misleading. The institutions are mere shells, hollowed out by the absence of economic rationality, and by the internal games played within them. They are pure fiefs. Weber has described the Chinese bureaucracy as patrimonial rather than rational-legal (Weber 1978). It always has been and it still is. Chinese modernization, then, has been, above all, an attempt to move up the formalization scale of Figure 2.2, firstly by adopting the bureaucratic trappings of a Marxist-Leninist order, and then later, when that failed, through an *ad hoc* and ill-understood emulation of early Eastern European reform models. Yet the culture, aided and abetted by the very irrationalities of the models borrowed so uncritically, constantly dragged the system back into fiefs.

One example will suffice. At various times during the 1980s, measures were enacted to decentralize state power to local authorities as well as to industrial firms. The major Chinese cities would retain a larger proportion of tax collected, of foreign exchange earned, and would generally have more scope to manage their own affairs without constant meddling from the centre. Industrial enterprises themselves would be allowed to hold on to their profits, would be allowed to develop off-quota production, and would gain some freedom in personnel management.

In practice what happened? In the absence of any institutions that could keep an effective check over the decentralization process things quickly spun out of control and the centre lost its grip. The powers granted to local authorities allowed them to reassert control over enterprises that were themselves supposed to become autonomous economic entities. These enterprises would be 'protected' by these local authorities from the 'chaos' (read 'competition') of the market in return for their 'loyalty' and obedience, the essence of the feudal contract and the fief.

In Eastern Europe the issue is quite different. There, a Marxist-Leninist structure was imposed upon industrialized societies that had already moved quite far towards a decentralized market order. A rational-legal bureaucratic foundation was already in place after the war, one which, to be sure, was badly damaged by it. If the logic of this structure – the soft budget constraint, investment hunger, etc. – also pushed towards informal face-to-face arrangements as in the Chinese case, it did so from a point located much higher up the formalization scale. After all, Eastern Europe participated in the broader European movement from *Gemeinschaft* to *Gesellschaft* (Tonnies 1887) that occurred over three centuries and which replaced the arbitrary exercise of personal power with that of role-based power. For this reason, communist centralization in Eastern Europe, for all its irrationality, was effectively experienced as an expression of bureaucratic power – albeit with frequent lapses into fiefdom – whereas in China it merely served to perpetuate an earlier feudal order.

The upshot of this analysis is that the managerial challenges facing foreign investors in Eastern Europe, in spite of similarities in the institutional structure, are quite different from those encountered in China. We turn to these in the concluding section below.

IMPLICATIONS AND CONCLUSIONS

Joint ventures are organizations that operate where secure market contracts cannot be written (Williamson 1975). They are devices for pooling risks and sharing the consequences whether positive or negative. The uncertainties that inhere in their operations are reduced by joint learning often over a protracted period of time. The uncertainties themselves may result from the characteristics of a market that remains undeveloped or untested, from a technology whose applicability is not yet established, from the vissicitudes of an institutional or cultural environment that is hard to understand, and so on. Partners are sought for their ability to reduce uncertainty and in the best cases they complement each other along some critical performance dimension.

A major element of uncertainty that joint ventures have to deal with, however, stems from the nature of the relationship that binds the partners to each other. Are their respective objectives clear and are they mutually compatible? Will these remain compatible as the collaboration evolves? Do the partners share enough common values to behave with mutual consideration in a crisis? and so on. All this points to the importance of trust and understanding between partners in the evolution of joint venture collaboration, and these are not built overnight.

The high rate of failure of Sino–foreign joint ventures, I would argue, has two main causes.

The first cause is that the cultural distance between contracting parties as measured by the distance between them in the space of Figure 2.1 is such that a great deal of time and effort would be required to get them on to a common wavelength. Recall that foreign respondents in the CEMI survey cited *internal* management problems far more frequently than external ones as stumbling blocks to effective collaboration. If the institutional logic of Chinese managers locates them in fiefs while that of western managers locates them in markets, then they will find themselves at opposite ends of the space in Figure 2.1. The implication may well be that on this basis, the joint venture is the *least* appropriate form of collaboration since the costs of learning and adaptation might prove too high for both parties.

The second cause is a direct consequence of the first: a gross underestimation by both the foreign and the Chinese parties of the time and effort required to build trust and understanding. Everyone is in a hurry to clock up results, even if these only figure on paper. A climate of intense competition has been fostered in which both sides are panicked into setting up joint venture arrangements the scale of which often outruns the joint learning and trust building necessary to their success.

In Eastern Europe, the problem of culture distance is likely to prove much more tractable than in China since the contracting parties are located more closely to each other in Figure 2.1. Getting on to the same wavelength should therefore not prove insurmountable.

Yet this process of mutual familiarization remains a crucial requirement for joint venture success, and unless the necessary time and effort is devoted to it, many a potentially fruitful collaboration could still come to grief.

If effective joint learning rather than quick profitability is accepted as the initial objective of the joint venture process in Eastern Europe then one implication becomes clear: initial investments should be kept small and only increased in size as learning takes place. Large investments lock foreign investors and local partners into situations that are hard to treat subsequently as a sunk cost if things do not work out. Small investments by contrast not only can be more easily treated as a learning cost but also have the added advantage of vastly increasing the number of eligible local partners that one could work with. Large investments will direct one towards existing or ex-state-owned enterprises with corporate cultures that may prove impossible to change; small investments orient one towards a new breed of domestic entrepreneurs who have had to learn, often painfully, how to beat the old system rather than yield to it.

Targeting small nimble-footed entrepreneurs makes a lot more sense in Eastern Europe than it ever did in China. There, the main contribution of a foreign partner is to help local firms move up the formalization scale, towards more effective bureaucracy rather than away from it. Small entrepreneurs in China are still at the bottom of the social and education ladder and are usually in no position to follow this path; they are typically Marx's 'petty commodity producers', eking out a living on the margins of society. In Eastern Europe, on the other hand, the challenge is less one of creating rational-legal organizations – these already exist to a far greater extent than in China – than of institutionalizing a process of decentralization both managerially inside the firm, and towards markets outside the firm.

Internal decentralization will be what large state-owned enterprises will be struggling to achieve both prior to and after privatization. Some of these will prove capable of change and hence make viable joint venture partners; most, in all likelihood, will not, and are destined to sink under the cultural weight of their own past. External decentralization will be the fruit of a competitive entrepreneurial process, of free entry and exit into product markets, of an emerging culture of risk taking and reward.

In China, with the exception of the Southern provinces, the large state-owned enterprise continues to be protected and shielded from bankruptcy by state supervisory bureaux at the expense of small entrepreneurs who lack social legitimacy. It can therefore make sense for prospective foreign investors to minimize their risks by tying up with state-owned firms since these have large safety nets stretched under them. In Eastern Europe, however, state-owned firms are unlikely to enjoy such security and are therefore likely to be better prospects for outright acquisition than for joint ventures. Small entrepreneurial firms, by contrast, with a record of survival and adaptation are more likely to be open to joint learning and will require a lower initial investment by prospective foreign partners.

The foregoing analysis thus leads to a simple conclusion. If you want to reform communism, as the Chinese leadership did, channel foreign investors into joint ventures with state-owned firms in order to strengthen them. If, on the other hand, you want to get rid of communism, as the new East European leadership – with a few exceptions – does, then channel foreign investors into joint ventures, and indeed other forms of collaboration, with small entrepreneurial firms. This will stimulate decentralization towards a market order while focusing the economy on the creation of new jobs rather than the preservation of old ones.

REFERENCES

Boisot, M. 1986. 'Markets and hierarchies in cultural perspective'. *Organization Studies* (Spring).

—— 1987. *Information and Organization*. London: Fontana.

—— and Child, J. 1988. 'The iron law of fiefs: Bureaucratic failure and the problem of governance in the Chinese economic reforms'. *Administrative Science Quarterly*, 33, 4 (December): 508–28.

—— and Xing, G. 1992. 'The nature of managerial work in the Chinese enterprise reforms: A study of six directors'. *Organization Studies*, 13, 2.

Campbell, N. 1988. *A Strategic Guide to Equity Joint Ventures in China*. Oxford: Pergamon Press.

Child, J. and Lu, Y. 1989. 'Changes in the level of decision making in Chinese industry: A window on the progress of economic reform 1985–1988'. Aston Business School Working Paper.

Dirkheim, E. 1933. *The Division of Labour in Society*. New York: Free Press.

Galbraith, J. 1967. *The New Industrial State*. Harmondsworth: Penguin Books.

Granik, D. 1987. 'The industrial environment in China and the CMEA countries'. in Gene Tidrick and Jiyuan Chen, *China's Industrial Reforms*. New York: Oxford University Press.

Hall, E. 1977. *Beyond Culture*. New York: Anchor Books, Doubleday.

Hendryx, S. 1986. 'Implementation of a technology transfer joint venture in the People's Republic of China: A management perspective'. *Columbia Journal of World Business*, Spring: 57–65.

Hofstede, G. 1980. *Culture's Consequences: International Differences in Work Related Values*. London: Sage.

Killing, P. 1982. 'How to make a global joint venture work'. *Harvard Business Review*, 60, 1: 120–7.

Kornai, J. 1986. 'The Hungarian reform process: Visions, hopes and realities'. *Journal of Economic Literature*, 22: 1687–1737.

National Council for US–China Trade. 1987. *US Joint Ventures in China: A Progress Report*. Washington, DC: US Department of Commerce.

People's Daily. 1989. 'Adhere to opening to the outside world', 3 October: 3.

Pugh, D., Hickson, D., Hinings, C. and Turner, C. 1969. 'The context of organization structure'. *Administrative Science Quarterly*, 14: 91–114.

Pye, L. 1985. *Asian Power and Politics: The Cultural Dimension of Authority*. Cambridge, MA: Harvard University Press.

Rostow, W. 1960. *The Stages of Economic Growth*. Cambridge: Cambridge University Press.

Ruggles, R. 1983. 'The environment for American business ventures in the People's Republic of China'. *Columbia Journal of World Business*. (Winter): 62–7.

Tidrick, G. and Jiyuan Chen. 1987. *China's Industrial Reforms*. New York: Oxford University Press.

Tonnies, F. 1887. *Gemeinschaft und Gesellschaft*. Leipzig: Reisland.

Warner, M. (ed.). 1987. *Management Reforms in China*. London: Frances Pinter.

Weber, M. 1978. *Economy and Society*. Berkeley: University of California Press.

Williamson, O. 1975. *Markets and Hierarchies*. New York: Free Press.

DISCUSSION OF MAX BOISOT'S PRESENTATION

Gay Haskins asked Max Boisot whether the diffusion process described in his model in effect meant that employees were being handed down codified solutions by managers who knew the answers.

Max Boisot replied that what employees might receive from managers was codified information which they then had to explore and play with in order to tease out of it both potential problems as well as potential solutions. This playing he associated with an absorption of codified data which, through a process of learning by doing, employees would internalize and subsequently gain competencies in scanning their environment and responding to it.

Marjan Cerar saw the information diffusion process as a cybernetic feedback loop in which the way that information flowed and got processed varied with its degree of codification.

In Eastern Europe, Max Boisot argued, the focus is exclusively on changing the institutional structures through which information is processed at present and in the language of the model on switching from a bureaucratic to a market mode. It is assumed that firms will adjust automatically to this switch. What the model suggests, however, is that the switch will only be successful if it triggers off a learning process *inside* the firm and such learning indeed requires the creation of multiple cybernetic feedback loops, not only to link the firm more responsively to its external environment, but also to connect its constituent elements to each other.

John Child asked how far the particular configuration of a firm's social learning processes and hence its position in the space of Figure 2.1 were dependent on its chosen strategy.

Max Boisot replied that effective organizational learning requires an organizational memory. Most firms attempt to secure such a memory for themselves by moving their organizational processes further up the formalization scale. Codified practices can be stored more easily in documents than uncodified ones. Yet codification only ever captures part of an organization's stock of knowledge. Much stays behind, locked up in the heads of certain employees. A firm pursuing explicit strategies, therefore, is likely to have a differently shaped learning trajectory in the space from one pursuing implicit strategies.

Tom Lupton argued that the choices expressed in the act of codification are very much a function of personal intuitive skills. Max Boisot agreed but felt that a firm that relied solely on uncodified intuitive processes would sooner or later experience a brake on its organizational growth. He cited as an example, the case of Sportis. The firm had clear potential for growth but could not exploit it because most processes and data were carried around informally in Thomas Holç's head. Only by moving up the formalization scale and creating explicit organizational systems will the firm be able to decentralize managerial decisions and grow.

Jane Salk stressed the need to maintain an ability to scan for uncodified data as one moved up the codification scale. The competitive environment is pretty turbulent and ambiguous at the best of times.

Max Boisot commented that effective learning requires the ability to develop information processing skills and structures thoughout the space of Figure 2.1. In Eastern Europe the focus was firstly restricted to the codified regions and then to the rightward shift from bureaucracies to markets. A more dynamic approach to organizational problems is required. Any strategy that relies solely on codified data rapidly degenerates into a mechanical planning exercise and will simply perpetuate the culture and organizational practices of the command economy.

John Child then asked what the implications of this view might be for a firm like Sportis.

Max Boisot hypothesized that entrepreneurs are constantly trying to escape the procrustean effects of a market order moving into the region of Figure 2.1 labelled fiefs. The fief region is a great source of personal power and identity for the entrepreneur and for that reason he seeks to dwell there as long as possible. But in doing so, he subsequently resists those further moves up the formalization scale which would allow his firm to grow. This was Steve Jobs's problem at Apple when he was running the Macintosh division and it might well be Sportis's main problem today. Entrepreneurs who in seeking to escape markets remain in fiefs for too long end up preventing their firm from growing through codification of informal practices and in effect become their own worse enemies.

Lee Vansina then wondered whether a truly entrepreneurial firm was in effect ever capable of becoming a learning organization. It may be doomed to remain entrepreneurial.

Concluding, Max Boisot thought that this would be so if 'entrepreneurial' were taken to mean dominated by an entrepreneur. In Figure 2.1, entrepreneurship is located in Fiefs as a phase in a continous learning process. Who plays what role in that phase will determine whether or not the firm gets stuck there. Eastern Europe's major problem is that large state-owned firms are culturally not equipped to move down the space of Figure 2.1 into the uncodified regions, whereas the small entrepreneurial firms are not managerially equipped to move up the space and there to build robust organizations.

Chapter 3

Case study one: Salamander and Lenwest

Anton Artemyev and Ian Turner

SALAMANDER AND THE OPENING OF EASTERN EUROPE

Introduction

Salamander A.G. is Western Europe's largest manufacturer of shoes with ten factories in Germany and France. Salamander is also the only manufacturer in Western Europe to offer a full range of shoes for men, women, children and infants. In addition to its manufacturing activities, Salamander also possesses a chain of wholly owned shoe shops in Germany and in selected locations eslewhere in Europe and the world.

History

In 1885 a young master shoemaker called Jacob Sigle set up his own workshop in Kornwestheim, a small town not far from the Swabian capital Stuttgart. Jacob was joined two years later by his brother Ernst. The Sigles' shoe business soon flourished, the product line expanded and the brothers' workshop soon became a small factory. In 1891 Sigle met a young travelling salesman called Max Levi. A talented salesman with experience of the shoe business, Levi agreed to throw in his lot with the Sigles and a new firm – J. Sigle & Company – was set up for the marketing of footwear. In 1897 Ernst Sigle visited America and returned to Kornwestheim to introduce American production methods. Already by the turn of the century the company was employing more than 400 workers and producing some 300,000 pairs of shoes per year.

In 1903 the company was approached by Rudolf Moos, a Berlin shoe dealer who in an effort to drum up trade was inviting tenders from shoe manufacturers for a new low priced men's boot. Sigle and Company took up the challenge and the resulting boot soon gained a name for itself. Moos had earlier patented the name and logo Salamander for shoe polish and in 1904 he extended this to cover footwear as well. Levi was quick to appreciate the advantages of a strong brand name like Salamander. One way of exploiting the brand was to open company-owned shoe retail outlets throughout the German Reich. This established the brand name in the consumer's eye and led to greater product differentiation, whilst stabilizing demand and making production planning easier. In 1905 Sigle and Company founded the Salamander Shoe Company jointly with Moos in Berlin. Moos subsequently sold his share of the business to the Sigles and in 1930 Sigle and Company was merged with Salamander to form the Salamander A.G.

Levi soon realized that Salamander could not rely solely on wholly owned retail outlets. These only became viable, they discovered, in towns with more than 100 thousand inhabitants. In an effort to buttress their forward integration policy and provide greater certainty of production in the long run, Salamander developed a system of exclusive franchising for towns with between 2,000 and 100,000 inhabitants. The deal was simple, Salamander gave frachise holders exclusive distribution rights for the term of their contract within the agreed locality. In return the franchise holders agreed to source exclusively from Kornwestheim within the price range laid down by Sigle. Each franchisee had also to meet an annual sales target laid down by Salamander.

Salamander's two-pronged marketing strategy through wholly owned outlets and franchised dealers provoked fierce counter-attacks from competitors but the first mover advantages were decisive and Salamander rapidly built a position as Germany's leading manufacturer and distributor of shoes. By 1939 Salamander had expanded its distribution network to encompass 126 wholly owned retail outlets in Germany and 1,882 franchise dealers.

Production at Salamander started again in 1945 after the Second World War and by 1967 the company was employing nearly 18,000 people with 18 manufacturing plants in Germany, France, Italy and Austria. In retrospect, this year marked the high point in the post-war development of Germany's shoe industry. Thereafter, output of shoes in Germany and other relatively high cost Western European countries declined as smaller shoe manufacturers were unable to compete against the invasion of low cost imported shoes from Italy and Spain. Salamander too was not unaffected by this threat and in an effort to reduce overall capacity several factories were closed in the early 1970s. In 1974 a new chairman was appointed to Salamander A.G. Dr Franz Josef Dazert set about modernizing production facilities to enable Salamander to compete more effectively and extended the company's distribution network. Dazert also broadened Salamander's strategy by expanding Salamander's wholly owned chemical works in nearby Turkheim, founded in 1969, and by building up Salamander's presence in France.

Salamander looks east

Starting in the mid-1970s, Salamander started to explore the opportunities for business in Eastern Europe. Clearly the closest of the former communist countries, both geographically and culturally, was the German Democratic Republic (GDR). In 1976 Salamander concluded the first in a series of contracts – called *Gestattungsverträge* – with the East German authorities which enabled East German shoe factories to produce shoes and shoe polish under the Salamander brand name as part of a licensing deal. The contracts were perennially renewed and Salamander shoes soon captured a large share of the East German shoe market. As payment for the licences, Salamander received shipments of East German textiles and clothing which it marketed in the West. Salamander's East German textile marketing operations were handled by three small subsidiaries based in Konstanz and Berlin. These operations generated sales of DM 70 million in 1990. Up until the start of 1990 when, with the unification of Germany, the contracts became invalid, Salamander had sold 50 million pairs of shoes under licence in East Germany. The jewel in the crown of Salamander's East German operations, however, was undoubtedly the exclusive rights which it acquired to market the famous Meissen porcelain in the West. Bock GmbH., a separate subsidiary based in Konstanz, generated DM 50 million of sales of Meissen porcelain in 1990. Following unification Meissen abruptly terminated the agreement with Salamander. Bock is to be relocated in Frankfurt am Main, where it will work closely with manufacturers in the former East German states and as a trading company for other international products.

Table 3.1 Turnover and growth within the Salamander Group, 1990

	Turnover in million DM	% Growth
Shoes	908.0	+1.3
Chemicals	94.6	+4.5
Technical services	120.8	+3.0
Other trading companies	207.2	+9.8
Total	1,330.6	+2.9

Structure

The Salamander group consists of four main business areas: shoes, chemicals, technical services and other trading companies.

As you can see from Table 3.1, shoes made up something like three-quarters of the Salamander Group's business in 1990. Table 3.2 lists the companies in the Salamander Concern. Most important of these is clearly Salamander A.G. which turned over DM 505 million in 1990 out of a Concern total of DM 1,227 million.

Strategic vision

Dr Dazert retired as Chairman of the Board of Salamander in 1989 and was succeeded by Gerhard Wacker. Wacker came to Salamander in 1985 following a career which had included positions in the Bertelsmann Publishing Group and latterly with Jacobs Suchard A.G., the Swiss chocolate manufacturer. Since his appointment as chairman of Salamander, Wacker has continued a policy of steady diversification away from shoes into less mature industries. This includes Salamander's holding in two companies specializing in industrial cleaning and decontamination. Wacker likes to characterize Salamander as a 'multiple specialist'. Wacker continues to see Salamander's future to be in the shoe industry, however, and much of his efforts have been centred on strengthening the company's position. HIs approach has first of all been to refocus Salamander away from being production-oriented to being more focused on marketing. At the same time, under Wacker's leadership Salamander has launched a number of new brands, such as the 'Camel' line in mens' shoes and the recently launched 'Orbit Nova' in ladies' shoes. These new brands together with the other lines of Salamander's own shoes represent one strand in the company's defensive response to the threat of cheap competition from foreign

Table 3.2 The Salamander Concern at December 1990 (thousand in local currency)

Sector	Currency	Exchange rate (100 local currency)	Equity	Shareholding
Shoes:				
Salamander Schuhhandelsgesellschaft mbH. Kornwestheim	DM		33,000	100.0
Salamander-Bund. GmbH. Kornwestheim	DM		28,160	50.0
Melvo-Vetnecs-Gesellschaft MbH. Kornwestheim	DM		2,130	100.0
Rovo Immobliien GmbH. & Co.KG. Konstanz	DM		1,079	100.0
Salamander Import-Export GmbH. Kornwestheim	DM		10,000	100.0
Salamander in Austria Ges.mbH. Kornwestheim	OS	14.212	90,276	100.0
Salamander France S.A. Paris	FF	29.39	42,906	100.0
Chemicals:				
Chemische Werke Salamander GmbH. Tursheim	DM		35,100	100.0
Other trade:				
Klawitter & co. GmbH. Konstanz	DM		21,503	100.0
Klawitex Import-und Export Handelsgesellschaft mbH. Berlin	DM		21,503	100.0
Verkauts-Agentur Klawitter GmbH. Konstanz	DM		5,703	100.0
Bock Manufaktur-Porzallane Handelsgesellschaft mbH. Konstanz	DM		7,256	100.0
Technical services:				
Deutsche Industriewartung GmbH-Co.KG Stuttgart	Dm		37,447	66.1
DIW Industriewartung Gesellschaft mbh. SL. Potten	OS	14.212	5,569	44.1

Source: Annual Report 1990

countries. Wacker hopes that these moves will improve Salamander's image and appeal and enable it to compete in the higher value segments away from cheap imports. (Whilst the name Salamander has always stood for quality shoes, in the past some of their products have been viewed as being rather dowdy.) The company is no longer able to produce shoes profitably for sale below the popular DM 100 price band (for men's shoes) and has had to reposition itself as a result.

Distribution

Salamander continues with its tried and tested formula of wholly owned distribution outlets in large towns and exclusive franchise operations in smaller locations. From the beginning of 1990, retail operations were separated out into an independent wholly owned subsidiary. Distribution and manufacturing are now to operate at arm's length and Salamander hopes that this will improve efficiency and encourage greater entrepreneurial initiative.

At the same time, the company has recently completed a programme of distribution rationalization with the closure of over 25 outlets in Germany and a further 20 overseas. At the end of 1990, the company possessed 170 wholly owned company shops in the Federal Republic and a further 1,750 exclusive dealerships. Outside of Germany Salamander had a further 88 company-owned retail outlets in France, Austria, Switzerland and Belgium and some 4,000 exclusive dealerships in Europe, North and South America, Africa and Asia.

Salamander's rationalization of its distribution network in West Germany was to some extent offset by the opening of a further 15 retail branches in the former East German states in 1991. In addition to direct sales to the public, Salamander also sold shoes in large volumes to public authorities, police forces and the army.

Production

Shoemaking is a complex industrial process. A shoemaker like Salamander could produce between 20 and 40 different styles at any one time, each of which would require between 30 and 40 operations in small batches on the same production line. Computer-aided design is now widely used in the shoe industry but attempts to automate the production process have not met with any great success and shoe production still remains a skilled and labour-intensive operation.

As Salamander itself points out, during the manufacturing process each individual operation (about 200 are involved), is directly related to finished product quality. Three factors are of prime importance: material, shape and workmanship. The repeated inspection procedures to which the materials are subjected at every production stage serve to guarantee that quality is maintained. Salamander's production values are high grade materials, international fashion flair, top quality workmanship, a perfect fit and comfort for the wearer.

In 1990 the company produced a total of 9 million pairs of shoes in all its various factories, up on the previous year's 8.2 million pairs. The impact of cheap foreign competition is also visible in the pattern of production. The majority of Salamander's uppers and over a third of the completed shoes sold under the Salamander brand in 1989 were manufactured abroad. For the same reasons, in 1989 Salamander closed two of its West European factories, one in Germany and the other in France. Output from these works is to be offset by production from joint venture operations in Hungary.

Investments

Although the shoe industry is a relatively mature industry, in order to remain competitive, investments are needed. Salamander continues to invest to the tune of DM 40 million a year. These investments included in 1989, DM 6 million for the modernization and rationalization of its plants in Germany, in addition to the DM 0.7 million invested in the joint ventures in the Soviet Union and Hungary. A further DM 7 million was invested in the modernization of retail outlets and the implementation of improved data processing and communications technology.

The chemicals area also received its share of investment at DM 12.5 million. This was used for the extension of production capacity for plastics and leather.

Personnel

The number of employees in Salamander A.G. continued to fall, reaching 3,260 in 1990 (this figure does not include sales staff in the companies' shops). This fall was mainly a result of the closure of the plants in Germany and France. Personnel costs accounted for some 86 per cent of the value added of Salamander A.G. in 1989.

Finance

As you can see from Appendix 3.2, Salamander's turnover has now recovered given a sharp dip in the late 1980s. This undoubtedly reflects the general malaise in the European shoe industry, due to the weakness of the US dollar in the period after 1987 (see below). However, although both turnover for the A.G. and for the Group as a whole grew (by some 11.5 per cent in the case of the latter), profits failed to keep pace. Thus the return on sales for the A.G. declined in 1989 to 4.4 per cent from 4.8 per cent in the year before. Further pressure on profitabliity came in 1990 with the conclusion of a new agreement with Salamander's workforce in Germany. The combined package of increased wages and reduced working time increased overall wage costs by some 4.5 per cent.

European shoe market

The latest crisis in the European shoe market began in 1987. Following the weakness in the US dollar, European companies found it much more difficult to sell their higher priced shoes in the United States. Exports of European shoes fell by almost a third, from 105 million pairs to 70 million pairs between 1986 and 1988. It also became less attractive for the newly industrializing countries like South Korea and Taiwan to export their shoes to the United States and so, almost overnight, these companies switched their attention to more accessible markets in Europe.

As imports of shoes into the EEC rose from just over 300 million pairs in 1986 to nearer 500 million pairs in 1988, at a time when consumer demand in these markets was levelling off, the European shoe industry was left reeling. By 1988, 42 per cent of the European market was taken up with imports from outside of Europe. In Germany import penetration rose to 93 per cent by 1989. Only Portugal and Spain seem to have remained relatively unscathed, due to their low cost base. Elsewhere, in France, Italy, Germany and the United Kingdom, jobs went by the thousand as companies either sought to rationalize in the face of this competitive onslaught, merged with other competitors or simply went out of business. Of the 461 companies which had belonged to the Association of the

German Shoe Industry in 1979, only 252 remained ten years later. Quotas imposed by some European states, notably France and Italy, proved ineffective in staunching the flow of cheap imports. The European Commission has so far resisted attempts to organize a European-wide quota against Asian shoe producers. The importers have since shifted their own strategy subtly. By 1990 the volume of imports from Korea and Taiwan was falling off, although the value was maintained through a consistent move into higher priced, higher quality leather footwear. At the same time, many of the Korean and Taiwan manufacturers set up shop in Thailand and Indonesia in order to beat import controls.

Germany continues to be Salamander's largest market (see Table 3.3) accounting for nearly 60per cent of Salamander A.G.'s turnover in 1989. Domestic sales of shoes in Germany have fluctuated considerably since 1986, not least due to the unnaturally warm winters in 1987, 1988 and 1989 which had an impact upon the purchase of Salamander's winter shoe collection. Consumption rose again in 1990 to 334 million pairs, 12 per cent up on the previous year, but domestic sales by German producers declined over 15 per cent. Salamander could not escape this trend. Its German turnover declined from DM 433 million to DM 417 million in 1989.

International business

Salamander owed the continuation of its expansion in the late 1980s, in the face of a drop in its domestic market, to its success

Table 3.3 Breakdown of turnover (DM 000,000) by sector and region

Turnover by sector	Konzern		Salamander AG	
	1990	1989	1990	1989
Shoes	904,668	940,957	505,288	730,871
Chemicals	94,635	90,521	–	–
Other trading	120,803	117,330	–	–
Technical services	207,251	188,825	–	–
	1,227,357	1,237,634	505,288	730,871
Turnover by region	Konzern		Salamander AG	
	1990	1989	1990	1989
Federal Republic	836,985	741,596	259,440	417,340
Other EEC countries	125,730	124,234	46,348	41,368
Other areas	264,642	371,304	199,500	272,163
	1,227,357	1,237,134	505,288	730,871

Source: Annual Report 1991

in overseas markets, principally those outside of the EEC. Exports to Eastern Europe currently make up a large part of Salamander's continued growth. Salamander continues to produce for sale in the Soviet Union. These are special purchases of shoes by the Soviet government. The Soviet government orders these shoes in advance and in order to smooth out problems of production and materials procurement, Salamander has in the past produced them well in advance of delivery and before the funds to pay for them have been transferred. With the recent problems over hard currency payments from the Soviet Union in mind, Salamander has reversed its previous practice of producing to contract in advance of payment and as a result, the working week was shortened in 1991 in four Salamander factories.

In the former communist states of Central Europe, Salamander's presence is most visible in Hungary, where in 1989 the company formed a joint venture with the largest Hungarian wholesale and retail distributor. The joint venture firm, Fonicia, a 50/50 joint venture, currently has over 50 retail outlets in the Budapest area. Salamander also has another joint venture in Hungary called Salamander Budapest whose function is to coordinate the various cooperative agreements with Hungarian shoe factories and to develop foreign trade activities. In Poland Salamander has opened a single retail outlet in the centre of Warsaw which it views as a way of establishing the Salamander brand name in the public eye.

Gearing up for business in Eastern Europe

Salamander decided to establish a separate company, Salamander Import/Export (Salimex) specially to handle business in Eastern Europe. In 1991 Salimex employed some 20 people: individuals chosen for their expertise in trade and business, as experts on specific countries in Eastern Europe and as linguists with two or three foreign languages of relevance to this area. Some of these people are actually stationed permanently abroad, for example, Salimex now has an office in Moscow with its own warehouse facilities which deals with sales and barter business. Ten employees are permanently located there, some of them on secondment from Salamander in Budapest.

THE FORMATION AND OPERATION OF LENWEST

Origins and rationale of the Soviet operations of Salamander

Salamander has had export contracts with the Soviet Union since the end of the 1970s. In 1980 Salamander opened detailed discussions with the Soviet ministries, primarily the Ministry for Light Industry, in order to establish the Salamander name in the Soviet market. The initial idea was that by producing shoes in the Soviet Union Salamander would gain sufficient favour with the Soviet authorities to make exporting directly to the Soviet Union safer and more stable. However, this idea turned out to be a non-starter because the responsibilities for allowing production in the Soviet Union and for purchasing goods outside the Soviet Union were divided between different ministries which did not necessarily see eye-to-eye with one another.

Out of these exploratory talks, however, grew the idea for forming the joint venture (JV) which was later called Lenwest. Salamander is the only western shoe company to have such a massive presence in the Soviet Union. Most European shoe companies are small or medium sized companies, without enough capital to become involved in long-term projects like the Soviet Union and without the market knowledge which a company like Salamander has gained through experience. From Salamander's point of view, the Soviet market represented a huge market which was not well provided for and had an enormous potential for the company. If Salamander could establish itself in that market in the same way it had in other markets, then Salamander's top management believed that it had to be successful. Apart from the strategic aim of exploring the vast Soviet market and promoting a brand with a view to future profits, a JV also offered Salamander the prospect of commercial returns in the near future from 'know-how' sales. According to the JV agreement, Salamander was to be paid DM 2 for every pair of shoes manufactured with Salamander technology. As far as the political risk was concerned, Salamander believed this could be contained. Even under a return to a communist government, there would be a need for shoes. The only difficulty that could arise would be if expropriation were carried out; even then the Russians would in effect be killing the goose that laid the golden egg.

The shoe industry in Leningrad in the mid-1980s

In the years before *perestroika*, the shoe market in the USSR was comparatively stable. The output of the domestic shoe industry was of low quality and limited variety, and customers preferred imported shoes. Nevertheless, Soviet shoes were readily available at all shoe retailers and their comparatively low prices ensured stable demand. From the mid-1980s there were increasing shortages of shoes in the shops. There were two main reasons for this. In the first place, there was an increase in demand for shoes along with other consumer goods. This was inevitable as income levels rose whilst the price of goods remained fixed at the same level. The second reason was the state of the shoe industry which was not capable of raising output to satisfy rising demand. The shoe industry in the USSR was subject to central planning and distribution of material and technical resources. The central authorities failed to make the necessary investments in the shoe industry. Investment in existing plants in the mid-1980s was only half the level it was twenty years before and no major plants had been reconstructed since the beginning of the 1970s. As a result, the volume of production was practically static and quantitative output targets were only met by increasing the proportion of light shoes (i.e. sandals, summer shoes, etc.). Annual ouput was approximately 850 million pairs, half of which were light shoes. The shortfall caused by the shortage of domestically manufactured shoes was made up by imports, mostly from East European countries, and approximately 400 million pairs were imported annually. The total potential demand in the domestic market, given an annual rate of consumption of 5 to 6 pairs per capita, can be estimated at about 1.5 billion pairs annually. In the mid-1980s the situation deteriorated further due to a continual drop in shoe imports linked to a general decrease in trade between the USSR and Eastern Europe and, more recently, to a shift to hard currency transactions.

In Leningrad Region the situation was no better than in the country in general. The shoe industry was organized within the framework of the 'Skorokhod' Production Association (annual output of about 30 million pairs) which was owned by the Ministry of Light Industry. Although about 2 per cent of the country's population lived in Leningrad Region and the local shoe industry manufactured over 4 per cent of all shoes made in the USSR, half of the output was distributed to other regions of the country and most of the rest was purchased by consumers from other regions of the USSR coming to Leningrad.

To the typical weaknesses of state-owned shoe enterprises in the USSR (i.e., out-of-date equipment, low quality of materials, production line methods, etc.), was added in the mid-1980s another negative trend: the centralized supply system began falling apart but without a new market system being created to replace it. All this meant that it was no longer possible to raise quality and increase the quantity of manufactured shoes within the framework of then-existing legal structures for economic activity. The Decree of the Council of Ministers of the USSR on JVs issued in 1987 (see Appendix 3.1) created the opportunity for radical change in this situation for those enterprises which were psychologically ready for it.

The situation at Proletarskaya Pobeda from the mid-1980s

At the beginning of 1987 Proletarskaya Pobeda ('Proletarian Victory') was a state-owned shoe manufacturing company with an annual output of approximately 6 million pairs of shoes for men, women and children. It did not differ much from other state-owned shoe companies in the Soviet Union. In 1986 it had separated from the 'Skorokhod' production association as a result of Skorokhod's expansion and was now directly accountable to the Ministry of Light Industry of the USSR. Despite the fact that state-owned enterprises are still less independent than, say, JVs, there have been many changes in their activity during the years of *perestroika*. Thus control by the Ministry of Light Industry of the USSR came to an end in 1990. In its place was coordination of the activities of shoe companies by the state concern 'Roslegprom'. At the same time state control over production was abolished along with price control. 'Regulated' prices were introduced, but only for certain types of product, like shoes for the elderly and old models of shoes.

Establishing the joint venture

The talks between Salamander and the Soviet authorities centred initially on agreements to do with the transfer of know-how through licensing or know-how agreements rather than joint ventures. Although these talks never came to anything, in the process Salamander came to know quite well a number of shoe factories in Russia. As a result Salamander developed good relations in particular with the Skorohod Production Association. The initiative to form a joint venture came immediately after promulgation of the decree on JVs in January 1987 from the Russian side. The Minister of Light Industry made the approach, remarking that as the talks on licensing had never come to anything, why don't they talk about forming a formal joint venture?

During the preparation period, Salamander made enormous efforts to analyse potential partners and assess the prospects for a JV. Salamander's brand name, in-house expertise and vast distribution network put it in a strong position. In the USSR, however, there existed many shoe enterprises with similar technology and equipment, many of which were visited by experts from Salamander before they made their choice.

The final choice of Proletarskaya Pobeda was determined by several factors. There were the traditional skills of Leningrad shoemakers, the availability of raw materials and semi-finished goods, and the existence of a plant with production capacity and potential for expansion. But, above all, it was the presence of young, energetic and enthusiastic managers which was decisive.

The Soviet partner was motivated primarily by the opportunity of expanding production which was not possible without setting up a JV. In this respect the JV form had a number of features which facilitated expansion:

- an independent investment policy;
- independence in choosing suppliers;
- low taxes during the launch period;
- access to modern technology and to Salamander's expertise in control and production
- hard currency revenues from exports via Salimex's distribution network.

Lenwest: stages of expansion

Since it was founded in October 1987, Lenwest, as the JV was called, has undergone several major stages in its development. During the launch stage, production facilities were reconstructed in an amazingly short time given the prevailing conditions, due to the support of the local authorities. The first site, with an annual production capacity of 1 million pairs of shoes, was supposed to be launched within 18 months. In reality it took only 12 months! Actual production started in April 1988 and the first sales took place in May the same year. As of 1991 its capacity is 1.5 million pairs of shoes per year. The second stage began in November 1988 when a further production site with an annual output of 1 million pairs came on stream.

The rapid expansion of Lenwest could have been even more impressive had it not been for some restricting factors. In a 'deficit' economy where sellers rather than consumers dictated terms, supplies of raw materials had become critical for Lenwest with its fast growing production. All raw material resources were distributed centrally to state-owned companies (according to some current estimates, the free wholesale market in 1989 was only 13 to 14 per cent of the total market). Furthermore, domestic raw materials were of low quality and did not meet Salamander's standards. Despite the fact that Proletarskaya Pobeda gave Lenwest some of its raw material allocation, there was no easy solution to this problem. Originally, approximately 90 per cent of semi-finished goods and 80 per cent of raw materials had to be imported. Whilst imports were a severe drain on the hard currency reserves of the venture, the unsatisfactory quality of the output prevented it from being exported. The situation called for immediate action to locate suppliers in the domestic market. To this end, Lenwest signed a contract for raw material supplies with the Ministry of Light Industry of the USSR. The Ministry delivered the essential supplies and in return Lenwest paid the Ministry 5 per cent above their usual value and gave a commitment to produce a certain quantity of shoes.

Creating an integrated concern

In a largely *ad hoc* fashion, Salamander stumbled upon a strategy of vertical integration at Lenwest which it is still pursuing and which, so far at least, has proved its worth. For example, Kursk Leather Manufacturers, the main supplier of Proletarskaya Pobeda, could not produce water-resistant leather. Its leather became soaked in some 15 to 20 minutes, whereas Salamander's standard was 120 minutes. In 1988 Lenwest signed a contract with Kursk Manufacturers to supply the know-how for water-resistant leather production. In order to tie in the supplier, Lenwest provided it with equipment and technology, purchased for hard currency, supplied it with shoes in exchange for raw materials and set contract prices for leather that were higher than state wholesale prices. A similar approach was taken by Lenwest with other suppliers (see Figure 3.1). Thus the Leningrad thread factory, Krasnaya Nit, is now able to meet international standards, and the Voronezh plant is able to produce materials for rubber soles to a higher standard.

A different policy was worked out by Lenwest towards the Leningrad Radishev Leather Production Association which had from the start been supplying Lenwest with small quantities of leather for insoles and linings which were not in great demand. The Association had been facing difficulties due to raw material shortages, obsolete equipment, heavy fines for breaching health and safety standards, etc. Its desire for integration with a successful enterprise like Lenwest is easy to understand, therefore. Lenwest, for its part, wanted to integrate because of the geographical proximity of the two enterprises and the quality of personnel at the Radishev Association. A joint programme for the Association's revival was worked out which included complete reconstruction of one of its plants (Komintern Plant) with the assistance of German experts and the construction by a western contractor of a new environmentally friendly plant to produce leather for uppers.

Salamander eventually came to the conclusion that if it were going to invest so much time and effort into improving associated or supplier plants, it might as well have a share in such enterprises. Thus by the end of 1988, out of the operational necessity for vertical and horizontal integration, was created a Concern which included Lenwest, a shoe manufacturing factory in Riasan, 200 km south-east of Moscow (later named as Riasan-West) and Leningrad Radishev Leather Production Association. Also in the Concern was Lenwest Export-Import, a foreign trade firm, and a state-owned distribution company, the 'Centre for Commerce', which distributes 85–90 per cent of the shoes Lenwest makes for the domestic market. Altogether the Concern employed 9,500 people in 1991.

The following figures demonstrate the importance of vertical and horizontal integration for Lenwest. By the end of 1991, Riasan-West is expected to produce 1 million pairs of shoes, mostly for children, using Salamander's technology. Its planned annual output capacity will eventually be 2.5 million pairs of shoes. At the end of 1991, Lenwest's third production site with an annual output of

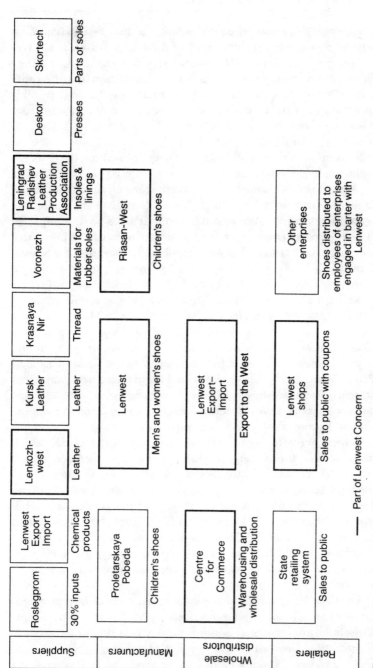

Suppliers								
Roslegprom	Lenwest Export Import	Lenkozh-west	Kursk Leather	Krasnaya Nir	Voronezh	Leningrad Radishev Leather Production Association	Deskor	Skortech
30% inputs	Chemical products	Leather	Leather	Thread	Materials for rubber soles	Insoles & linings	Presses	Parts of soles

Manufacturers			
Proletarskaya Pobeda	Lenwest	Riasan-West	Other enterprises
Children's shoes	Men's and women's shoes	Children's shoes	

Wholesale distributors		
Centre for Commerce	Lenwest Export–Import	
Warehousing and wholesale distribution	Export to the West	

Retailers		
State retailing system	Lenwest shops	Shoes distributed to employees of enterprises engaged in barter with Lenwest
Sales to public	Sales to public with coupons	

—— Part of Lenwest Concern

Figure 3.1 Vertical and horizontal integration at Lenwest, 1991

1.5 million pairs will come on stream, so that then Riasan-West will be producing over one-third of the Concern's output. Over 40 per cent of Lenwest's requirements for leather is satisfied from within the Concern. This formal integration and the other measures taken to integrate suppliers informally made it possible to reduce imports of semi-finished goods and raw materials from 80–90 per cent during the first year of operation to 5 per cent (mostly chemical components) by 1991.

In addition to the supplies Lenwest gets from within the Concern and from its suppliers, Lenwest obtains about 30 per cent of all its supplies from the Roslegprom concern, formerly the Ministry of Light Industry, at a price 15 per cent higher than the going rate within Roslegprom. Lenwest has also purchased some equipment and spare parts from other JVs, paying part of the price in hard currency. For example, Lenwest has obtained dies from the Soviet-German JV 'Deskor' and parts of soles from the Soviet-Italian JV 'Skortech', both situated in Leningrad. The Concern is still trying to sort out a current problem with the supply of certain chemical components, which still have to be imported. A hold-up in supplies from Armenia caused a shortage of latex used as a shoe glue. The Concern is also looking at the possibility of acquiring or coming to arrangements with other factories, including the Riasan Chemical Plant. Alternatively, the Concern could construct a new plant from scratch. There are limits to integration, however. The German partner believes it would not make sense, for example, to acquire chemical plants simply to secure supplies of glue.

If there were to be an economic reform in the USSR which introduced a functioning market system, then Lenwest might reconsider its approach to integration. However, in the short to medium term, vertical integration is the preferred route. In any case, the real problem is not the absence of market conditions but the lack of know-how in the supplier factories. Even if a market economy is introduced, this know-how would still be deficient and operations would have to remain vertically integrated until such time as the technology was transferred and the quality was up to scratch.

The lack of production facilities remains a serious problem. Lenwest put a lot of effort into getting a permit from the municipal authorities to construct a third production site in Leningrad. Despite this, Lenwest is still not able to produce a full range of shoes; children's shoes continue to be produced at Proletarskaya

Pobeda. Lenwest's plans to construct a new leather manufacturing plant are even more problematical. Despite the fact that the plant would have a full range of waste purification facilities, the City Government has not yet allocated a construction site. And finally, another major difficulty faced by Lenwest is the lack of warehouses to store the finished shoes.

The performance of Lenwest

Apart from its rate of growth, Lenwest differs from state-owned shoe factories in the quality and range of goods produced. Whilst the nominal productivity rate at Lenwest of 5 to 6 pairs of shoes per employee a day is practically equal to that at Proletarskaya Pobeda, the quality standards approach those at Salamander. This is due to the high quality of raw materials and semi-finished goods, the changeover from production line to individual processing and the tough technological controls. Lenwest is much better equipped than other shoe companies in the USSR. The machine pool is made up of German-made tools (Pfaff and Schoen), although most of the pressing equipment is Soviet-made.

Intensive efforts have been made to expand the range of shoes produced by Lenwest from 28 in 1989 to over 70 items in 1991. The collection is renewed every year following approval by the Board. The target set by the Board is to develop 50 new models each season. Accustoming employees to frequent model changes has proved more challenging from the management's point of view than introducing new technology.

To ease the introduction of new technology, every year 20 to 30 technicians and supervisors attend short training courses at Salamander factories in Germany. Courses are usually linked to the introduction of new models. After completing the course, these people return to retrain personnel in Leningrad.

The pace of work at Lenwest is much greater than in the average Soviet plant. Salamander introduced new personnel practices in order to attract and retain skilled employees despite the two-shift working schedule and the intensity of work. The average monthly salary at Lenwest of 800 roubles is more than double the Soviet norm and is higher than at other shoe factories. Employees also enjoy free meals and receive either a holiday bonus of 500 roubles or a free place at a recreation centre. Annual leave is 24 days which is also longer than in state-owned companies. Lenwest also makes loans to young families of between 5,000 and 20,000 roubles to help build their country cottages or dachas, or their apartments. As a reward for long and dedicated service, the Concern pays for 80 per cent of the loan.

The excellent performance of Lenwest would not be possible without close relations based on trust between the Soviet and German partners and embodied both in written and oral agreements. According to Mr Nosov, a member of the Board of the Lenwest Concern, the relationship is one of partners and colleagues not of 'teachers' and 'pupils'. Both sides have a lot to learn from each other, although the German side has a great influence on matters of technology and international marketing. This certainly affects personnel policy, but differences between German and Soviet employees are gradually becoming less marked. The degree of trust between the partners is typified by the fact that short–term liabilities on either side can be up to DM 5 million at any time. Of course, things have not always gone that smoothly. In 1988 Salamander sold a consignment of about 50,000 pairs of shoes on the Soviet market for hard currency via the foreign trade firm Raznoexport. The prices were slightly lower than those set by Lenwest and this led to some friction. The differences were soon smoothed out, however, and since that time, Salamander, Lenwest and the other JVs have agreed not to compete against one another with the same models. Of course, there are many other day–to–day difficulties. Thus, according to Mr Nosov, it is difficult and sometimes impossible to explain sudden changes in Soviet legislation, especially concerning taxation, to his German partners.

Marketing and distribution

In a deficit economy companies do not have marketing problems. Only when they start to do business internationally do they need to apply marketing principles. It was not originally planned to export shoes from Lenwest due to the limited volume of production. However, in September 1988, a special committee of Soviet and German experts judged that Lenwest's output had reached international standards and so the first batches of shoes were exported. Of the 1,120,000 pairs of shoes produced by the start of the second stage, 150,000 were sold abroad, in Finland, Germany and Iceland, using the Lenwest trademark and Salamander's distribution network. It is worth mentioning that JVs are not subject to the restrictions governing state companies on the export of consumer goods.

Finding a balance between foreign and domestic market sales has been a major issue for Lenwest. Of course, hard currency exports are attractive for Lenwest. But exporting large quantities of shoes will lead to competition with Salamander. Besides, it does not make sense to ignore the huge unsaturated domestic market either from a marketing or a social point of view. Moreover, the contracts Lenwest has with its suppliers require large numbers of shoes to be produced for barter transactions on the domestic market.

Out of 2.5 million pairs of shoes Lenwest sold in 1990, approximately 10 per cent was exported, mostly to Germany at DM 50 per pair; 15 per cent was sold for hard currency on the domestic market at contract prices, which, as a rule, are somewhat lower than export prices.

Initially foreign sales were distributed by Salamander using the Lenwest trademark; more recently Lenwest has been producing under the 'Mayer' brand for the Mayer chain of shops in Germany as well as a variety of shoes and boots for men under the 'Misha' brand and for ladies under the 'Celest' brand. 'Misha' and 'Celest' are also used in the Soviet Union.

As already mentioned, due to a lack of warehousing facilities, most of the wholesale distribution is carried out by the Centre for Commerce which is paid 6 per cent of the final retail price for its services. Retail sales are organized through Lenwest shops and the state-run retailing network, as well as through direct contracts with plants and factories in Leningrad. Lenwest's approach to opening up the Soviet market relies very heavily on the successful formula developed by Salamander. The setting up of the wholly owned Lenwest shops in places like Leningrad is something which stems from the Salamander philosophy and tradition of owning shops. However, in Russia consumers can only purchase Lenwest shoes if they also have a special coupon. The coupon system was a response to the storm of consumer interest when the shops were originally opened. To avoid panic buying or black marketeering, coupons are now distributed to organizations like old people's homes and veterans' organizations to enable them to purchase shoes. Human ingenuity being what it is, there is now a black market in Russia for the coupons as well! The basic problem is a shortage of shoes in the USSR. At the moment, Lenwest has six wholly owned shops in Leningrad. The plan was to buy about another twenty shops from the state, but a lack of clarity over the pace and direction of privatization has held things up.

Since the local market is unsaturated, most of Lenwest's output (about 80 per cent) is sold in Leningrad or Leningrad Region, and Lenwest's shoes are in any case ideally suited to the local climate. Nevertheless, other parts of the Soviet markets are being analysed, and business relations have been established either through agents or third parties in the Baltic states, Central Asia and the Ukraine.

Prices for the domestic market are set by the Board of Lenwest. Originally, the price of a pair of Lenwest shoes was about 60 to 80 roubles, corresponding to prices of similar imported shoes set by the state. After the price rise in 1991, which increased the prices of all consumer goods by two or three times, the average price of a pair of Lenwest shoes is 150 roubles, slightly higher than shoes made by state companies, but much lower than the market clearing price. The black market price of Lenwest shoes is several times higher than the official price in spite of the fact that the approximate average salary in the USSR is only 400 roubles. According to Mr Nosov, the Board sets the prices so that Lenwest shoes are in the medium price band. This is the main plank of Lenwest's marketing strategy. Lenwest plans to increase its production in order to combat the black market.

Financial performance

Lenwest had a turnover of about 92 million roubles in 1990. Tax on turnover for JVs was introduced on 1 July 1990. It affected the domestic sales for roubles of certain consumer goods. For shoes, the tax amounted to 25 per cent of the turnover in retail prices after deducting the cost of distribution and transport. At the same time, export/import taxes for the JVs were introduced. They do not affect exports of shoes, but can seriously hamper imports. Import taxes on synthetic fur, for example, amount to several hundred per cent.

Despite such tough taxation, total profits, calculated as the difference between revenues and costs plus turnover tax, amounted to 44 million roubles in 1990, and profitability, expressed as the ratio of profits to costs, was over 120 per cent. Profits of 10 million roubles were distributed for the first time in 1990 between the partners to the JV in proportion to their share in the JV's statutory capital. The rest of the profits was allocated to the

Funds for Production Development, Work Incentives and Social Development. Lenwest's parents had agreed that no profits would be paid out during the first three years. Money from the Fund for Production Development has also been invested in the development of supporting businesses, mostly Lenwest's suppliers, and in the development of the facilities at Riasan.

Bearing in mind the price rise and the increase in production, the turnover in 1991 is expected to be about 280 million roubles. From 1 January 1991, Lenwest is also liable to a 5 per cent sales tax, including sales of any imported goods. This tax is similar to V.A.T. in the West. Worse still, on 1 April 1991, the three-year tax holiday which Lenwest had initially enjoyed as a JV came to an end. Since then the JV has been paying 25 per cent of its profits, after allocations to the Reserve Fund and the Fund for Production Development, to the Russian Federation.

The introduction of these taxes in 1990/1 could have resulted in increased prices for children's shoes, so the Concern began negotiations with the Ministry of Finance of the USSR, and an agreement on favourable taxation for Riasan-West was being drafted in summer 1991.

Rigorous taxation has has not yet damaged Lenwest's financial positon, however. In 1991 the JV's assets were over 110 million roubles and current profitability (return on costs) despite rising costs remained very high at about 80 per cent. Returns on investment at Lenwest were estimated at over 40 per cent in 1990/1. Only once, in 1988, has Lenwest had to use external financing when it took up a loan of DM 5 million for three years from Vnesheconombank, in order to pay for imports of raw materials and semi-finished goods. The loan has been paid back and all current expenses and long-term investments are now funded internally. The volume of exports at DM 30 million annually also exceeds imports by DM 20 million. This healthy financial state allows Lenwest to carry out social sponsorship programmes of 2 million roubles annually. These include financing the construction of waste purification facilities at power plants, acquiring medical equipment and medicines for children's hospitals and making welfare payments to pensioners.

Shareholding arrangements and management structure

On 15 October 1987, Lenwest was registered with the Ministry of Finance of the USSR. The Statutory Fund was shared between

Proletarskaya Pobeda (60 per cent) and Salimex (40 per cent) in accordance with the official exchange rate used by the State Bank of the USSR. The JV's original Statutory Fund amounted to approximately 3.5 million roubles, 2.1 million in roubles and 4.2 million in DM. The Soviet party to the JV contributed imported and Soviet equipment and physical assets for the reconstruction of production facilities to the Statutory Fund; the German party contributed equipment. According to the accounting rules governing JVs, reinvested profits prior to January 1990 are viewed as part of the Statutory Fund. Due to allocations of retained profits and to new investments by the participants, Lenwest's Statutory Fund increased to 12 million roubles by 1991, divided 51/49 between the Soviet and German partners. Due to the increased interest of Salamander towards Lenwest and by mutual agreement, Salamander took over the Salimex share in Lenwest from 1 January 1991.

Having transferred part of its production facilities to Lenwest as its share in the Statutory Fund, Proletarskaya Pobeda reduced its production capacity from 6 to 3 million pairs a year. Of these, about 400,000 pairs are ladies' shoes and the rest are for children. This level of production has been stable throughout the last few years and only support businesses like production of heels and lasts are being developed. The Soviet partner is increasingly being hollowed out by the JV.

As an act of deliberate policy, Salamander took only a minority shareholding in Lenwest, preferring to leave the Russians in a position of responsibility. 'The Russian partner must have at least as much interest in the success of the joint venture as the Western partners have', Salimex chief Werner Rost explained. This involvement was extremely important, for example, with the procurement of material and labour in the Soviet Union. As Salamander sees it, there is a division of labour between the Russian and German management within the joint venture. The Germans concentrate on everthing to do with technical know-how, production facilities, machinery, training, distribution and marketing. The technical direction of the joint venture is in German hands and there are three Germans permanently resident in Leningrad at Lenwest. In addition, other German expatriates are deployed in Lenwest in areas like computing or accounting for shorter periods. The Russians, on the other hand, concentrate in particular on the procurement of raw materials and inputs. The Russians have developed, through many years experience, great skills at organizing materials, usually through compensation trade with other factories, so the Germans do not become involved in this. The Russian management also deals operationally with the whole question of recruitment of personnel, although top management appointments are done in agreement with the German partners.

The management structure is capped by an administrative council or Board which has a similar function to a supervisory board in German law. This consists of five people, three of whom are Russians, including one representative from Roslegprom. The other two Russian representatives are from 'Proletarian Victory', whilst the two German representatives are, of course, from Salamander. The Chairman of the Board is a Russian, Mr Kolovai, and the Deputy Chairman is Herr Rost, a member of Salamander's management board and, as head of Salamander Import-Export, responsible for the company's strategy in Eastern Europe and the Soviet Union. The Board meets every three months in different locations. Its purpose is to set the general strategic direction for the joint venture. The day-to-day management is in the hands of the Soviet General Director, responsible for production, and a German Deputy Director, responsible for new models and technology. In practice, all the operational decisions are taken jointly by the Deputy and the General Director. Under them is a German Technical Director and Russian managers in charge of Sales, Logistics and Purchasing and Personnel. The General Director does not sit as of right on the Board but he can be summoned to present reports to the Board and receives a copy of the agenda.

With the formation of the Lenwest Concern, a separate management structure had to be created. All members of the Concern are legally independent and joined the Concern on different financial conditions. Riasan-West was formally acquired by Lenwest's parents and, along with Lenwest Export-Import, is a wholly owned subsidiary of Lenwest. Radishev Association joined the Concern on the basis of business cooperation to carry out joint leather development and production programmes. In addition, another JV, 'Lenkozwest', was set up by Radishev Association (50 per cent), the German leather company SUS (32 per cent), established by Salamander and Schafstall, and Lenwest (18 per cent). The Centre for Commerce remains a wholly state-owned company and joined the Concern on the basis of business cooperation. (See Figure 3.2.) The Board of the Concern comprises Mr Kolovai, as

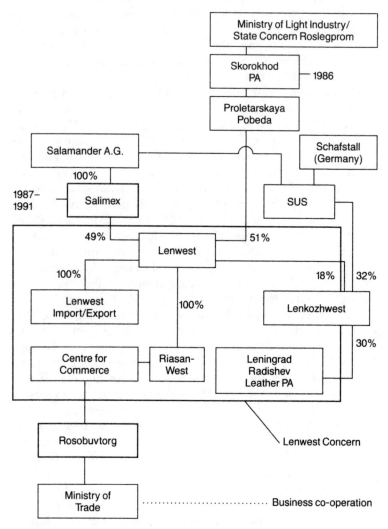

Figure 3.2 The structure of the Lenwest Concern, 1991

President, Mr Nosov and Mr Melikhov, Director General of a company in which the Radishev Association has a share, and, on the German side, Herr Rost and Herr Franke, Technical Director of Lenwest.

Expanding activities: the formation of Belwest

In 1988 Salamander followed the successful establishment of Lenwest with another Soviet joint venture – Belwest – situated in Byelorussia. Again, the initiative came in the same way from the Ministry of Light Industry of the USSR which wanted to establish production sites for shoes in all the various Soviet Republics. By that stage Salamander had already had one year's experience of working in Lenwest. The company believed that the Lenwest concept was going to be successful and it could be repeated in the case of Belwest, provided they could find a factory which had suitable managers and a reasonable production capacity.

Because Belwest was situated in another Republic, it was not possible to integrate it within the Lenwest Concern, so Salamander had to establish a separate joint venture. In other respects, however, the company pursued the same model as it had done with Lenwest. Some of the problems, however, were different. For example, the supply situation was better in Lenwest, situated as it was in the centre of a large industrial shoe complex, than it was in Belwest. Belwest suffered due to the disintegration of the Union, because it was situated in one of the smaller Republics where there were fewer supplying factories. On the other hand, as a result, the morale and the feeling of sticking together was, if anything, greater in Belwest.

The future

Changes in the political and economic system in the Soviet Union will clearly have a profound effect on the future development of Lenwest. Some steps towards a market economy have already been taken. By 1991 there were over 300 commodity exchanges in the country. The state still dominates retailing, but privatization is on the way and the share of goods sold at free prices is constantly increasing. In foreign trade the monopoly of the Ministry for Foreign Economic Relations has been abolished. Controls on trade remain through registration of foreign trade activity and licensing of export-import operations, but a Decree of the Russian government issued in July 1991 allows anyone, including individuals, to have access to the external market.

This means Lenwest can now carry out both production and trading activities. For example, the Centre for Commerce, apart from selling Lenwest shoes, also markets imported shoes from

Vietnam and Hong Kong and shoes manufactured by Proletarskaya Pobeda, and Lenwest Export-Import exports goods like timber, animal skins, etc. to Germany. So far trading operations consitute only 5 per cent of Lenwest's turnover, but according to Mr Nosov, it could make up as much as one-third of the turnover. The Concern is analysing the activity of the various exchanges in the USSR and there are plans to set up a brokerage firm within the Concern or to collaborate with other brokerage companies.

The other main change in the business environment will be the move to rouble convertibility. The 'official' exchange rate in 1991 was $1 = 0.60 Rbs. A so-called 'commercial' rate of $1 = 1,8 Rbl was introduced for JVs in November 1990. In April 1991, in addition to these rates a fluctuating rate – the 'tourist' rate – was introduced and is set by the State Bank at $1 = 32 Rbl, roughly in line with black market rates. However, the monopoly of the state on hard currency operations is constantly being eroded. From 24 July 1991 all commercial banks have the right to sell currency purchased at the tourist rate. Since 1990 the State Bank has held frequent hard currency auctions for companies including latterly JVs and foreign investors.

There are clear indications, therefore, that a hard currency market is being formed and will result in a market exchange rate of the rouble, regulated by supply and demand. Rouble convertibility will, of course, highlight the immense gap between export and domestic prices. At a black market rate, Lenwest export prices are several times higher than those used on the domestic market.

Finally, Lenwest's future depends on the new laws governing foreign investment and the creation of free economic zones. A Presidential Decree of Foreign Investments was issued on 26 October 1990, announcing certain guarantees and safeguards for foreign investors. Foreign investments in the USSR are to receive the same legal protection as Soviet companies. Profits made in the USSR in roubles can be reinvested or spent in the USSR or transferred abroad. The decree also gave the go-ahead to establish free economic zones in the USSR.

This decree was implemented by laws adopted in the USSR and Russian Federation in July 1991, thus creating a more favourable legal climate for foreign investments. In order to promote the growth of JVs, the registration procedure was also recently simpli- fied, allowing the Republics and certain large cities like Leningrad (now St Petersburg) to register JVs on their own.

These changes will clearly create a new competitive environment for Lenwest. Up to now Lenwest has had practically no competition in Leningrad. Market entry by foreign companies, including Salamander, could seriously alter the situation. For example, Salamander has set up a branch office in Moscow independently of Lenwest. Lenwest has the advantage of being located in the Leningrad free economic zone. The Decree of the Russian Government in July 1991, setting up the Leningrad free economic zone, provided for, among other things, favourable taxation and customs duties, simplified registration procedures for joint ventures and licensing of export-import operations.

But the formation of the free economic zone could also be a threat to Lenwest. Shoe manufacturers from South-East Asia could import shoes into Leningrad or produce locally, competing with Lenwest on price. The liberalization of the economy and the disintegration of the old Soviet Union will present Lenwest with a number of challenges:

- Should Lenwest focus on its core business or diversify into trading operations?
- Does it make sense to change the legal and organizational form of the Concern, making it a public limited company, in order to raise funds to meet the threat of competition?
- Should it keep to its existing marketing strategy and pricing policy?
- Should it concentrate on its domestic market or seek to expand its business abroad, and if so, in which countries?
- What should be the form of its future relationship with its German parent, Salamander?

As for Salamander, it intends to continue and consolidate its activities within the Soviet Union. Apart from Lenwest and Belwest, Salamander is keeping open options in other Republics within the Soviet Union, although this is a question of capital and in particular, of investment of hard currency which at the moment is in short supply. Salamander's approach is to take things slowly in the current political climate. Nevertheless, it too will face a number of strategic challenges in the future:

- Will the market in the Soviet Union continue to be more attractive for Salamander than other investment opportunities?
- Will the formation of wholly owned subsidiaries in the Soviet Union offer a better risk-reward ratio than JVs.

- What should be the future relationship between Salamander and Lenwest? Should Salamander integrate Lenwest within its worldwide operations, perhaps as a separate brand at a lower price point, or should Salamander and Lenwest adopt a geographical division of labour?

Whatever the answers to these questions, Salamander and Lenwest's record speaks for itself. A substantial JV has been formed and operated in a difficult period. Perhaps this represents a model which other businesses could follow?

APPENDIX 3.1

Joint ventures in the USSR: a brief summary

Long before *perestroika* many western firms had started doing business with the Soviet Union, mostly selling goods to Soviet Ministries and state-owned companies for hard currency. However, until 1987 there were practically no direct foreign investments in the USSR. The Decree on Joint Ventures issued in January 1987 was intended to attract western capital with new technology, know-how and means of production to the USSR, to serve a domestic market suffering from permanent shortages and to reduce the need for imports. JVs were intended to have:

- a high degree of independence from state management;
- direct access to the domestic and international markets.

The joint ventures were to promote entrepreneurship in Soviet managers who would be fully responsible for the JV's survival.

The apparent growth of JVs is impressive. Only 23 JVs were registered in 1987 and a further 168 in 1988. But about a thousand were created in 1989 and some three thousand in 1990. The total turnover of JVs, estimated at around 1.1 billion roubles in 1989, increased four times in 1990. Hard currency sales on the domestic market have increased from around 200 to 650 million roubles. Exports have gone from 126 to 283 million roubles, whilst sales for roubles have increased from 842 to 3,435 million roubles, which indicates that JVs are becoming domestic market oriented.

However, there is another side to this. The JVs' share of Soviet GNP is much less than 1 per cent. Their imports, financed mostly by loans from Vnesheconombank of the USSR, have increased from 420 million roubles in 1989 to 940 million roubles in 1990.

As a result the share of JVs in the Soviet balance of payments deficit is over 10 per cent. Originally intended to be sources of hard currency, or at least self-financing in currency, JVs became a major cause of hard currency outflow.

This may prove to be a temporary phenomenon associated with the launch stage of JVs, but nevertheless, the trend is of some concern.

Joint capital invested in JVs by the end of 1990 was estimated at some 6 billion roubles. Thus the average Statutory Capital of a JV in the Soviet Union is several times smaller than in JVs established in developed countries. At the same time, the degree of diversification in Soviet JVs is comparatively high. On average, every JV is engaged in four fields of activity. For western businessmen, this is seen as a way of reducing risk. The number of JVs registered in the last quarter of 1990 suggests a decrease in western businesses interest. According to some estimates, only one quarter of the total number of JVs registered were operational by 1991. The rest were not operational mainly because western partners had not made the necessary investment in the JVs' statutory funds.

JVs are established mostly in sectors where there is a great demand in the Soviet market, like light industry, consumer goods and timber, or in the sectors that do not require massive investments, like services, consultancy, publishing, production of video and audio materials, assembling of PCs and software production. Thus the development of JVs in the USSR has so far failed to meet the original aspirations of the Soviet authorities. There are several reasons for this, which can be roughly divided into two main groups. The first group encompasses the political, economic, institutional and legal aspects. Firstly, there is the problem of the unconvertible rouble. In recent years this has been the main obstacle preventing western partners from receiving profits in hard currency, although the situation is improving. A Presidential Decree issued in October 1990 allows foreign investors to convert their rouble profits into hard currency and repatriate the latter. A further problem is the political instability in the USSR, especially as regards relations between Federal and Republican governments. And, there are, of course, difficulties with supplies of all kinds of materials, especially fuel and energy resources. In addition, there is a whole array of different legal and tax problems. Taxation can be a real problem for foreign investors in the USSR. Since 1990 there are new taxes on exports, imports and turnover. JVs with less than 30 per cent share of western capital are also liable to the same tough taxation applied to state-owned companies. Then there are the restrictions on foreign trade, including the ban on exporting goods purchased from other companies, the necessity to follow Soviet standards in book-keeping and accounting, which differ considerably from those used in the West, the inefficiency of the banking system, especially in regard to hard currency operations, and the lack of modern communication systems, to mention just some of the main difficulties.

The second group of problems includes all the administrative, cultural and organizational problems, like differences in management style, values, traditions, previous experience, language, etc. It is worth mentioning the importance of working out an agreed corporate strategy: the interests of the JV partners should at least not be contradictory, even if they do not always coincide.

All these problems explain why so few JVs are fully operational. Even so, there are a number of profitable and fast growing JVs in the USSR which lead one to hope that the original aspirations for JVs may not be totally in vain.

APPENDIX 3.2

Salamander in figures (Dm 000,000)

	1990	1989	1988	1987	1986
Group turnover	1,330.6	1,293.2	1,167.4	1,196.8	1,271.8
Concern turnover	1,227.4	1,237.6	1,110.1	1,123.2	931.5
Investments	50.4	39.5	28.8	29.0	42.2
Depreciation	27.7	31.9	35.1	36.9	29.2
Results of ordinary business activities	57.7	45.1	42.7	29.7	37.4
Annual trading surplus	25.0	28.7	22.7	16.4	18.2
Equity	336.5	328.4	312.3	261.5	238.2
Total assets	719.7	685.6	678.3	640.6	544.3
Number of employees	8,507	7,999	8,747	8,999	6,956

Salamander A.G.*

Turnover	505.3	730.9	649.1	681.4	736.2
Investments	45.9	11.1	19.4	14.1	33.3
Depreciation	7.4	13.5	16.2	13.4	17.3
Results of ordinary business activities	37.1	32.2	31.2	27.4	28.4
Annual trading surplus	17.9	20.9	16.6	15.6	16.0
Dividend	14.9	14.9	11.6	11.6	11.5
Dividend in DM per DM 50 share	9.–	9.–	8.–	8.–	8.–
Equity	285.0	282.0	272.1	226.1	222.2
Total assets	539.2	530.1	522.1	467.3	442.7
Number of employees	3,258	4,798	5,349	5,741	6,351

Source: Salamander Annual Report 1990
* Results for 1990 are not directly comparable with previous years figures due to the separation of the retail business into an independent company.

DISCUSSION OF ANTON ARTEMYEV AND IAN TURNER'S PRESENTATION

Jane Salk was struck by the vagueness of the joint venture agreement between the partners. So much appeared to be implicit and left to be dealt with as matters arose. Josip Skoberne stressed that no more in the USSR than elsewhere could joint ventures be considered a panacea to the difficulties that currently confront state-owned firms. He pointed to major differences in the interests of the investing parties. The western investor was using the joint venture as a learning platform and for this reason was willing to take a long-term view; the local partner, by contrast, was often just responding opportunistically and under short-term pressures – to secure inputs no longer available locally, to get better technology, to find export markets, etc., in short, to survive.

Ian Turner felt that the western partner's long-term orientation should not obscure the fact that in the USSR he still had to be pretty well self-sufficient. Parent company support was a fragile reed indeed on which to build up a successful joint venture. The local operating environment simply did not allow such support to be available in a timely fashion.

Imre Spronz echoed this view, adding that many Hungarian firms had experienced problems in running joint ventures in the USSR. He felt that Soviet partners have an oversimplistic view of what joint ventures are all about. The firms of post-communist countries should certainly invest in the USSR – the opportunities over the long term are excellent and these firms have much to offer, but they should not necessarily turn to joint ventures as the ideal investment vehicle.

John Child felt that from the point of view of the host country, joint ventures have a lot to offer. The VW joint venture in Shanghai, for example, served as an important role model for Chinese state-owned firms and exerted great pressure on local suppliers to upgrade their performance. From an exchange between Anton Artemyev and John Child, it transpired that the Lenwest joint venture appeared to be less subject to state interference that most Chinese joint ventures and to enjoy a greater degree of managerial autonomy in consequence.

Max Boisot wondered whether role models might create more harm than good in many cases. More often than not they stimulated the kind of imitative learning that John Child and Livia Markoczy described in their presentation: little genuine understanding on the part of the imitators is gained as to why things are performed one way rather than another. The Chinese joint venture landscape today is littered with the debris of mindless imitation.

The discussion then turned to the institutional environment in the USSR. Marjan Cerar wanted to know who on earth he was supposed to negotiate with given the current changes. Anton Artemyev replied that today it would not be with ministries. In fact, he recommended that in spite of the official institutional safeguards created to attract foreign investors, under current circumstances they would be well advised to go slowly.

A similar situation had plagued foreign investors in China, Max Boisot noted, when the state delegated a number of powers to provincial and city governments in the early 1980s. Many western firms, having invested heavily in building up contracts within the central bureaucracy, were then caught with their pants down.

Jan-Peter Paul claimed that his firm was eager to enter the Soviet market but that the institutional situation there bordered on anarchy. There were no clear guidelines, no credible laws. Taxation policy varied from area to area and appeared to be arbitrary. Joint ventures required a credible legal environment for their development. In its absence, all talk of governance is empty.

Summarizing the discussion, Max Boisot observed that the attitude of some state-owned firms in communist or post-communist states – China, Poland – was reminiscent of a Melanesian cargo cult: the locals wait around for a big, magical, iron bird (usually a

DC4) to bring them precious gifts. Socialist economies share with many Third World countries a particularistic orientation, a concern to bring about specific outcomes rather than a concern with rules. Market economies are more universalistic, that is to say, rule governed. If joint ventures are required to operate in a particularistic institutional environment, there is a danger that they could exploit it to their own advantage and thereby acquire an interest in perpetuating the old order rather than in changing it. For this reason, changes in governance at the corporate level call for changes in the governance of other institutions. Failing this, joint ventures could easily have counterproductive effects.

Chapter 4

Case study two: Tianjin Nutrexpa Food Company

Manuel Vallejo and Max Boisot

INTRODUCTION

On 24 September 1991, Mr Samaranch, President of the International Olympic Committee, presided over the inauguration of the Tianjin Nutrexpa Food Co. Ltd (for summary details see Appendix 4.1), the first joint venture in China of Nutrexpa SA (Spain), sponsoring company of many sporting events in Spain.

The inauguration was the culmination of an effort that had started in 1985. Three and a half years of negotiations and of endless to-ing and fro-ing by both the Chinese and the Spanish partners in the proposed venture had been followed by a two-year start-up phase, and by September 1991 the joint venture had in fact been operational for about half a year, albeit unofficially.

Things had not been easy, for apart from the notorious difficulties encountered by western firms working in the Chinese commercial environment, the economic turbulence generated by the leadership's many policy gyrations had been compounded by the impact that the Tiananmen massacre of June 1989 had had on the confidence of foreign investors. Had the world misjudged the country's future development direction? Would foreign firms find their investments beached by the receding tides of economic reform?

In spite of the obvious risks and the doubts, Nutrexpa decided to push ahead.

BACKGROUND

Like many foreign firms before it, Nutrexpa had been attracted by the glittering prospects of the Chinese market. From its first initial steps in economic reform in 1978 and through to its industrial reforms of October 1984, China had successfully projected itself as the most progressive and pragmatic of the communist economies. With its decision to open itself to the outside world and to abandon the Maoist quest for self-sufficiency, China seemed to be telling prospective foreign investors that ideology would not be allowed to stand in the way of economic development and the measures necessary to achieve it. Indeed many of the reforms it embarked upon – the development of a legal system; allowing an increase in the autonomy of enterprise managers; the creation of market oriented Special Economic Zones (SEZs), etc. – were explicitly devised to convince such investors that putting their money behind China's modernization was no more risky than investing in any other LDC.

Nutrexpa was receptive to the message implicit in the country's new policy orientation. With over a fifth of the world's population, a per capita milk consumption that was abnormally low even by developing country standards, and a policy commitment by the government to increase both the production and the consumption of milk, China represented a long-term market opportunity that was hard to match and that Nutrexpa, with its wide international experience in production and management, was well placed to respond to.

But how? The firm was well aware of the pitfalls that awaited foreign investors in a country so unfamiliar with western commercial and financial practices. Many of the larger Sino-foreign joint ventures – Beijing Jeep, Volkswagen, the Occidental coal project, the Sheraton–Great Wall Hotel – were currently in difficulties that owed far more to the behaviour of the Chinese partner or the state agencies that supervised him than to any problems with the domestic market.

Nutrexpa, nevertheless, resolved to push ahead and to build up its activities, but to do so slowly. In its approach to the Chinese market, it was guided by two general principles:

● to think small and to invest incrementally while the local environment was being mastered and understood. By avoiding large-scale investments buttressed by voluminous feasibility studies, the firm could in effect remain proactive and flexible without exposing itself to unacceptable financial risks.
● to capitalize on this gradual mastery of the local environment and to build up the confidence of its local Chinese partner. A

relationship of mutual trust and respect between the partners would provide an important foundation for future growth.

The company's approach might thus be described as one of fostering a process of mutual learning.

In the Chinese economic environment that prevailed, however, mutual learning promised to be a slow business. Negotiations for the joint venture, for example, were begun in the spring of 1985 but the contract was not signed until September of 1988. The negotiating team on the Chinese side lacked suitably trained people, those that were found were constantly switched around, and on several occasions, the negotiation process stalled completely.

Furthermore, an eagerness to sign up foreign joint venture partners at the central government level did not necessarily translate into a similar eagerness at the local level. Typical problems encountered were:

- divergent objectives of the partners: the Chinese joint venture partner was much more interested in selling inputs to the joint venture – i.e. a cocoa bean press machinery line, cocoa powder, etc. – than in actually helping the joint venture sell its own outputs.

- different evaluations of the joint venture partners' respective contributions: Nutrexpa was to contribute US $1 million worth of machinery and US $0.1 million of foreign currency for its 50 per cent share, and the Chinese partner was to contribute buildings and land use rights valued at US $0.5 million and working capital valued at US $0.7 million. Yet, since there is no market in land in the PRC, land use rights are valued by the local authority in ways that would strike a westerner as arbitrary and self-serving. And since working capital is almost impossible to determine accurately using socialist book-keeping methods – it has been estimated that over 90 per cent of Chinese state-owned firms work with distorted figures – the cash value of the local partner's contribution was also hard to establish.

- the inablity of the Chinese partner to make good his contractually agreed contribution in land use rights because of urban planning restrictions imposed by the very local authority that happened to own the firm.

- the reluctance of the Chinese partner to pay for intangible property rights such as a trademark license or to accept territorial restrictions on the commercial distribution of the product. Until the country opened up to foreign investors, intangible property rights – patents, trademarks, brands, etc. – were unknown in China. Chinese managers considered it the most natural thing in the world to 'borrow' successful brand names, ideas, trademarks, etc. and were often quite perplexed by restrictions placed by foreign investors on what they considered to be 'free goods'

Problems encountered during the negotiation phase were resolved by a mixture of flexibility – Nutrexpa, for example, decided to accept a postponement of the Chinese partner's working capital contribution – and tenacity – the Spanish director's salary was not included in the final agreement as it would have given rise to demands for an identical salary for the Chinese director, a practice established in other Sino–foreign joint ventures.

THE STARTING-UP PHASE

The starting-up phase lasted from October 1988 until September 1990. It was a period of discovery and adjustment in which the many challenges of working in the Chinese environment quickly became apparent and seemed to justify the slow incremental approach adopted. Below are listed some of the many issues which the Spanish General Manager, Manuel Vallejo, had to deal with over the period.

• Finding a Chinese director and vice director acceptable to both joint venture parties proved more difficult than expected. The Spanish side was looking for someone with something of a western managerial profile and the capacity to act autonomously on his own initiative to ensure the profitability of the venture. The Chinese side was looking for someone subservient to its own interest in the joint venture. This was not necessarily profitability. Chinese motives for entering into joint venture arrangements with foreign investors have usually been many and varied – prestige, access to foreign exchange and to imports, more favourable treatment by the supervisory authority, priority allocation of scarce supplies, etc. – and profit as such has usually not ranked high among them. As it happened, the Chinese firm that was partnering Nutrexpa was not rated very highly by the Tianjin local authorities, and at one point, its president and director were both dismissed by the authorities for 'internal' reasons. Clearly, in the Chinese institutional environment, the power of shareholders – particularly if these were foreign – was not what it was in market economies.

- It proved more difficult than anticipated to recruit foreign workers. In the early days of China's economic reforms, workers had flocked to Sino-foreign joint ventures: wages were often up to twice what were paid in domestic state-owned firms and the level of bonuses and other benefits were also much higher. To be assigned to a joint venture was thus considered a privilege to be treasured; it was much sought after.

But there were costs associated with such work and word soon got around that these sometimes outweighed the benefits on offer. The first of these concerned work norms. The pace of work in the typical state-owned firm is anything but demanding. A power cut, a failure of deliveries, poor scheduling of work – all daily occurrences in most firms – quickly bring work to a standstill, so that three hours of actual work in a typical eight-hour day strikes the average worker as being in the natural order of things. When it became known that foreign investors expected eight full hours of work for eight hours of pay, many workers considered the deal as verging on exploitation.

But the volume of work turned out to be only half the story. Foreigners also expected workers to show initiative and to be willing to take responsibility for their decisions. In an institutional environment where the most minute details of a worker's – or indeed a manager's – activities were specified either by state regulations or by a supervisory agency located outside the firm, it was hard to socialize workers to the idea that they had both the right and, indeed, the obligation to make decisions for which they would subsequently be held accountable. Personal freedom and responsibility have been neither much sought nor prized in the Chinese state-owned enterprise.

The work norm that caused the most panic, however, was the one that sanctioned dismissal for poor quality work or lax work discipline. One of the founding pillars of the communist state, and perhaps the one on which it its legitimacy ultimately rested in the eyes of the working population, was the provision of cradle to grave job security for workers. The capitalist labour practices enacted by Sino-foreign joint ventures were thus anathema to prospective Chinese recruits and the idea that they could actually be dismissed after a trial period filled them with dread.

- Establishing a unified management system proved difficult. The Chinese partner to the joint venture was reluctant to grant Manuel Vallejo the managerial discretion he needed to run the joint venture. There were two reasons for this. The first was cultural pride. Chinese people felt that they had been pushed around too much by foreigners up until the time that the communists came to power and they were thus psychologically unprepared to 'take orders' from them even if this was required by the logic of the situation or by the terms of a joint venture agreement. Giving direction and managing thus proved to be a permanent process of negotiation and persuasion.

  The second was institutional. Managerial discretion in the Chinese state-owned enterprise is a privilege claimed by the firm's supervising bureau or by other state agencies located outside and above the firm. The director of a state-owned firm, even a large one, typically has little more discretion than a first-line supervisor in a western enterprise. Thus western joint venture managers expecting to exercise their managerial pre-rogatives in China often meet perplexity and puzzlement from those they work with. The role they expect to play has effectively no institutional counterpart inside the Chinese firm.

- Getting production under way proved an arduous business. The approval of budgets or their revisions by the Chinese partner was slow and since many activities gave rise to extra payments, delays were incurred. Another important source of delay was the central planning mechanism in China. Under the state plan, state-owned enterprises were allocated a certain quota of raw materials which matched what they were required to produce under the plan. Since the reforms, however, only part of these firms' total inputs and outputs were explicitly subject to the planning mechanism, the balance being obtained or disposed of in the market. The result of this dualism was arbitrage on a massive scale as firms sought to secure their own inputs at subsidized prices under the state plan but then sought to dispose of them at market prices which reflected their true scarcity. Many joint ventures which had been promised secure inputs of raw materials at guaranteed prices thus found themselves having to hunt around for their supplies and purchasing them at prices well above their original budgets. The Nutrexpa joint venture proved no exception to this rule and suffered important delays as a consequence.

• An interesting issue concerned distribution and promotion. Chinese state-owned firms had little need of marketing or advertising until the economic reforms. Given that, in a communist economy, consumer and producer goods are in perpetual shortage, a firm can usually sell everything that it produces with little difficulty, whatever the quality. Since consumers are offered no competing alternatives – competition was deemed to be 'wasteful' before the reforms – they are more or less compelled to take what is available. Under such circumstances a firm has no need of marketing: it simply hands over its output to a state distributor who then mechanically allocates it according to the provisions of the plan. With guaranteed sales the firm has little incentive to improve quality, to bring out new products, or to capture new customers.

The enterprise reforms, by allowing a firm to hold on to its profits, gave state-owned enterprises an incentive to increase their share of the market and to win new customers. In the newly competitive climate, foreign joint venture partners with marketing and distribution skills had much to offer state-owned firms. Two considerations, however, limited the full exploitation of these skills. The first was that most state-owned firms, having no concept of the role of marketing, consistently tended to undervalue marketing and distribution skills, preferring instead to focus on the foreign partner's technological contribution. Chinese industrial firms were exclusively production organizations and so, for them, the secret of a successful product resided exclusively in how it was produced. Marketing in this view was not even selling, it was order taking.

A second reason why a foreign partner's marketing skills could not be fully utilized had to do with the almost total absence of adequate market data on a national scale. Local authorities did not carry out market research as such and possessed consumption data only for their own districts. Since state-owned firms were expected to meet the needs of their own district first, most of them treated sales in other parts of the country as 'exports' – exports which in spite of the reforms frequently encountered fierce protectionist resistance from other local authorities concerned to preserve the local market for their own enterprises. Thus even a western firm would experience difficulty in getting a clear picture of the Chinese market as a whole. It was often confronted with a collection of micro markets, each of which had to be tackled on its own merits.

BECOMING OPERATIONAL

A number of the problems discussed above spilt into the operational phase and exerted systematic effects upon the joint venture's early performance. Production levels, for example, were extremely low at the beginning. There were difficulties in getting an adequate supply of plastic jars and labels at an acceptable level of quality and the price of sugar soared, reflecting the hoarding practices of suppliers faced with the possibility of getting free market prices for it. Production machinery kept breaking down, partly due to poor maintenance and partly due to the indifference of an unmotivated labour force.

Then the inability of the Chinese partner to make his working capital contribution as set out in the joint venture agreement led to a scarcity of working capital and to the need for a bridging loan, a problem compounded by a scarcity of foreign exchange needed for the purchase of imported inputs.

Also, finding competent personnel and devising incentive systems to motivate them that would be acceptable to the Chinese partner – steeped as he was in a culture and ideology of egalitarianism – was to be a continuing problem for the Nutrexpa joint venture as for most other Sino–foreign joint ventures.

Finally, a number of marketing problems surfaced. It proved hard to establish contacts further down the distribution chain with retailing units, or to secure exclusive distribution rights. Competing products appeared in the market whose performance owed more to the efforts of industrial espionage directed against Nutrexpa by other Chinese firms – often with the active connivance of the local authority in whose territory the joint venture was located (after all, were not joint ventures supposed to act as 'role models'?) – than to any intrinsic merit those products might have.

In spite of such difficulties, performance gradually improved, easing the early cash flow problems experienced and allowing the bridging loan to be paid off. The product found a ready acceptance among Chinese consumers and sales levels steadily increased. Competing products turned out not to be much of a threat on account of their poor quality and faulty brand positioning.

Soon the joint venture was initiating a second production shift with notable gains in productivity. The firm's profit and loss statement soon felt the benefits of such improvements which were enhanced by unexpectedly prompt payments by clients – this, in fact, was hardly surprising, since in a command economy plagued by constant shortages, the supplier, not the customer, is king.

Things were soon progressing fast enough to envisage entering the Shanghai market and to begin exporting Nutrexpa products back to Spain in order to earn some much-needed foreign exchange.

The talk today in the Nutrexpa joint venture is of doubling production capacity.

THE FUTURE

Nutrexpa's strategy is to treat its Chinese joint venture as an incremental learning experience on which it can build in the future. A problem solved constitutes a gain in operational capacity that increases the confidence of the local partner. The attitude of Nutrexpa is that this can only contribute to the process of joint learning on which the success of its China strategy depends.

APPENDIX 4.1

Brief profile of the Nutrexpa joint venture

Location:	The city of Tianjin, 120 km south-west of Beijing – a city of 8 million inhabitants.
Partners:	Nutrexpa, S.A., Spain: 50 per cent Limin Factory, Tianjin: 50 per cent
Capital contribution:	Nutrexpa: US $1 million in machinery US $0.1 million in foreign currency
	Limin: US $0.5 million in building and land use rights US $0.7 million in working capital
Purpose of joint venture:	The manufacture and commercialization of cocoa derivatives (in beans and powder – specifically *Cola Cao*) as well as honey ones.
Duration of joint venture:	Fifteen years with an option to renew.
Manufacturing capacity:	The machinery contributed by Nutrexpa is capable of producing up to 2 million kilograms per annum, in three shifts.

Number of employees:	Production	19
	Commercial	8
	Administrative	4
	Director and Vice Directors	4
	Personnel and services	8
	Total	43

Governance: Six directors of which:

The President and Vice Director are Chinese. The Director and Vice President are Spanish. The Directors of Production, Finance, Marketing and Personnel are Chinese.

DISCUSSION OF MANUEL VALLEJO AND MAX BOISOT'S PRESENTATION

Gay Haskins asked Manuel Vallejo whether, now that he was working on a joint venture in Poland, his Chinese joint venture experience would serve him in good stead. Manuel replied that it would but only to understand with the benefit of hindsight a mistake that had already been made in Poland. He pointed out that the products produced by the firm's Polish joint venture were being launched at almost the same time as those produced by the Chinese joint venture. Yet the Chinese launch had been five years in the making. The Polish venture was being operationalized much faster than the Chinese one and was consequently plagued with problems. The reasons for this are highly instructive.

In China, the firm knew that it was moving into a radically different cultural and institutional environment. Problems encountered by foreign firms working in China were well known and Nutrexpa had adapted its expectations accordingly, allowing plenty of time for a learning process to take root. In Poland, by contrast, the frame of mind with which the firm approached the venture was quite different. After all, this was Europe and thus a culture that the firm felt it already knew. Accordingly, and unlike in China, it delegated considerable responsibility for launching the new product to its Polish partner, a state-owned firm. This turned out to be a big mistake: the Polish partner, as might be expected by anyone familiar with socialist state-owned enterprises, had no clue how to launch a product. Clearly, it is the difference in Nutrexpa's own attitude towards the cultural environment that it operates in that explains the differences in its performance of its two socialist joint ventures.

José M. Anzizu observed that success in the Chinese environment required an unusual blend of patience and toughness combined together in a low-key approach. Max Boisot accounted for this requirement by the almost total absence of a credible legal framework in the country. What was in place had been installed largely to try to convince foreign investors that their money would be safe on Chinese soil. In fact, foreign investment success in China, as in the case described by Jan-Peter Paul for the Soviet Union, was predicated on an ability to build up personal relationships, a common understanding, and a large fund of good will by the Chinese partner and other Chinese stakeholders. For this, one either had to be large and rich or small and nimble-footed. Many small Hong Kong firms are of the latter type, and, like Sportis in the USSR, are able to operate profitably throughout China in the absence of any viable institutional framework, largely because of their intuitive understanding of Chinese culture and of Chinese ways of doing things. Hong Kong entrepreneurs, however, for the most part keep well clear of the Chinese bureaucracy or the larger state-owned firms.

Ian Turner asked Manuel Vallejo why it was so important to Nutrexpa to have a majority ownership in the joint venture. In the Lenwest joint venture in the USSR, for example, the German partner had not wanted a majority share (see the case by Anton Artemyev and Ian Turner, Chapter 3).

Manuel Vallejo replied that a majority share prevented all sorts of hassles with the Chinese partner. Nutrexpa had wanted to have the managerial authority and power to control the joint venture. Interestingly enough, though, after five years of collaboration with the Chinese partner, sufficient common experience and trust has been built up to make the question of managerial control a non-issue; the Chinese partner today is quite willing to let Nutrexpa have 85 per cent of the joint venture if it so wishes.

Anton Artemyev asked why Nutrexpa had not taken 100 per cent of the company. To which Manuel Vallejo replied that as a manager he had wanted the Chinese involved and working *with* Nutrexpa rather than *for* Nutrexpa.

In his summing up, Max Boisot thought he saw a common thread running through Manuel Vallejo's presentation and those of other joint ventures that the Round Table had been hearing about: if the foreign partner is able to use a joint venture as a learning platform more effectively than the local partner, that is, if it can learn about the local environment faster that the local partner can learn about foreign management practices or foreign technical practices, then gradually over time, the terms on which the joint venture operates move in the foreign partner's favour.

This phenomenon has been studied elsewhere and goes by the name of the *obsolescing bargain*. Given differential learning rates, a joint venture can often only be a temporary arrangement between partners, to be eventually discarded by the party that has learned the most the fastest. In such cases, the interests of the slow learning party cannot be fully safeguarded through the governance structure itself but must be pursued through the development of an appropriate strategy. In other words, the bilateral form of governance found in joint ventures can only serve to safeguard a *limited* number of joint interests – an adequate return on investment, transparency of performance, etc. – shared by the partners, and cannot be used to secure the full range of each party's long-term strategic interests. The protection of the latter requires the development of strategic thinking and skills. The most that a properly functioning governance structure can hope to achieve is to give these free play where they exist.

Chapter 5

Case study three: Sportis

Max Boisot

SYSKI'S SOLILOQUY

Michal Syski, Sales Manager of Sportis, chuckled to himself as his car reached the outskirts of Marki, 20 kilometres outside Warsaw, where his firm's headquarters were located. The journey to work had given him the time to savour the irony of Sportis's current situation.

Here they were, a small private concern employing little over three hundred people, barely one year after the Polish 'Big Bang' in which prices were freed up and the zloty devalued, facing the total collapse of their traditional domestic market. And what does Sportis do about it? Recognizing the necessity of developing its activities outside Poland in order to survive as a firm, in one bold leap it enters the one major foreign market in which it knows itself to possess a strong competitive advantage: not that of the US, Japan, or Western Europe, of course – what chance would a small Polish firm like Sportis stand there? – but that of Poland's former political master, the Soviet Union. By western standards Sportis may be lacking in funds and in know-how, mused Syski, but as this move shows it certainly is not short on entrepreneurship. No Sir.

Of course, he continued, westerners have always considered it difficult to work with the Soviets – differences in culture as well as in economic philosophy were sure to cause difficulties. But, he believed, perhaps the Poles had the necessary flexibility to succeed there where westerners might not.

And the people problem was by no means the end of it. The joint venture agreement which Syski had signed on 2 March 1991 on behalf of Sportis had as Soviet partners the fishing company, Murmanrybprom, and a garment repair firm called Silouhette.

Both were located in the city of Murmansk, some 200 miles north
of the Arctic circle. The last time Syski was in town, the temperatures were 45° centigrade below zero. No place for the faint
hearted.

Oh well, reflected the sales manager as he passed through the
company gates, so many barriers to entry against western competition. After all, which US, German, Japanese or British company
in their right mind would brave this frozen desolation, the ana-
chronistic caprices of 'Old believers', and the now galloping
entropy of the Soviet business system, in pursuit of a market
which, if anything, was probably shrinking? Had not Gosplan just
announced that domestic production had dropped by 11 per cent
last year, and was it not common knowledge that in Sovietspeak
11 per cent really means 16 per cent or more, making due allowance
for the duplicity and ignorance of central planners?

But as any Pole worth his vodka will tell you, pursued Syski,
gently stepping on the brake, a shrinking market is not bereft of
profitable opportunities. It may not offer much sustenance to a
Siemens or an IBM, but it is a square meal to a Polish firm of three
hundred people that is 'streetwise' in the Soviet Union and knows
where to look. Like many Poles, Syski felt he had got to know the
Soviets, their way of thinking, and their priorities, pretty well.
Geography had made the two countries neighbours and history had
provided numerous opportunities to get acquainted – not always
happy ones.

Many Polish firms had come to realize that in spite of the recent
demise of COMECON and the Soviets' lack of hard currency, the
Soviet market remained potentially a huge one for them (see
Appendix 5.1 for another brief example of such a firm) and,
paradoxically, for the very reasons that made the market unattrac-
tive to western investors: everything there is scarce and consumers
are therefore not too choosy about quality. Western standards of
quality are a luxury well beyond their foreign exchange allowance
and, more generally, their financial reach. Polish, Czech, and
Hungarian goods which would not be given shelf space in sophisticated western markets, are well received and often much sought
after in the Soviet Union. For East European firms that have the
patience and the flexibility such a market could be theirs for the
taking.

Sportis certainly had the patience and the flexibility needed,
thought Syski, but he wondered, under current circumstances,

does it have the stamina?. As he pulled up in front of his office, he could not help recalling that Sportis's remuneration for its minority participation in the Murmansk joint venture would be in fish – even dividend payments in the Soviet Union take the form of barter. How many clothing manufacturers in western countries can list fish on the balance sheet as part of their current assets and still stay in business, he asked himself.

SPORTIS: ORIGINS AND GROWTH

Life could be somewhat bleak for recently graduated young engineers in the Poland of the late 1970s and early 1980s. Although they were required to work for a state-owned enterprise for a minimum period of three years as a condition for studying at all, they knew, upon entering their respective firms, that unless they were prepared to sign up with the party and then bind themselves tightly to the *nomenklatura*, they were headed for nowhere as fast as their talents would carry them there. To preserve their sanity and that minimum level of motivation that imparts meaning to life, many resorted to moonlighting in those many eddies of the command economy that the state plan majestically sails by. Others, less concerned with job security, simply took time off.

So it was with Thomas Holç, a recent graduate in electrical engineering, who at the age of 20 was spending most of his time sailing and generally messing about in boats instead of crouching over a drawing board, as he should have been doing, designing lighting equipment for an obscure state engineering company. During his stolen leisure hours – and of these, at least, there was no shortage – Holç developed a great many contacts in the world of sailing and gained some insight into its functioning. He resolved that when he was released from his current servitude, he would put this clandestine experience to some profitable and, hopefully, enjoyable use.

Although Poland at the beginning of the decade did not offer a particularly hospitable environment for such heretical entrepreneurial thoughts – martial law was only a few months away and the economy, weighed down with external debts, was taking one of its periodic nose-dives – there were discernible signs of a new attitude towards private business by the authorities, albeit one forced upon them by the dire circumstances that they then confronted. As far back as 1976 legislation had been passed encouraging the creation of private business in Poland by foreigners of Polish origin. Thomas Holç had a brother, Andrew Holç, living in London, who would be willing to 'front' for him should it be decided to try something in this new climate. In 1980, therefore, Holç started collecting market data on a casual basis as well as investigating manufacturing processes. He did not have much money to invest at the time, but after seeing other budding entrepreneurs chancing their hand and subsequently succeeding, he decided to have a try with an initial investment of one million zlotys and one thousand pounds sterling. Sportis was created in 1983.

Shortly after the firm's creation, Holç came across an old ruin in the small village of Serock some 30 kilometres outside Warsaw, not far from a lake on which he used to sail. The local authority was willing to let him have the ruin for a nominal rent of two US dollars a month on condition that he restored it to its earlier condition. Once renovated, it was to be Sportis's first production facility.

Holç had originally intended to manufacture sails and life-jackets there and these primarily for export, but he was thwarted in this strategy by small far-eastern producers, located mainly in Hong Kong, who were able to sell a finished product on the world markets for a lower price than what he could acquire his inputs for in Poland – courtesy of the state pricing system. Yet since the renovation of his new building was now nearing completion, and local staff had already been recruited and were being trained, Holç felt under pressure to get going with something, even if that something was not quite along the lines he had initially envisaged. Was not the ability to adapt, after all, the essence of entrepreneurship? Thus it was that for the first nine months of its existence Sportis found itself in the business of making trousers.

Gradually, however, the firm was able to shift to the manufacture of life-jackets as originally planned, but now for the domestic rather than the export market. Its product offering consisted of fairly basic designs, mostly lifted from catalogues, whose colours and shapes were slightly modified to suit the requirements of the Polish market. The Polish navy turned out to be an important customer for these life-jackets, but the firm soon branched out into new product areas such as windproof clothing, tracksuits, windcheaters, etc.

Although Sportis was directly in touch with some end users such as the country's sea rescue services – 70 per cent of its sales at the time were in life-jackets – the bulk of its clients were state distributors such as Interster, Stoteczne Przedsiebiurstwo Handlv, Wewnetrzengo and Handlomor, or state owned or funded sports clubs acting as distributors. Itself having little or no direct contact with the market, the firm was unwilling to anticipate it and hence to invest in producing for stock. It would therefore only manufacture to order. Given the nature of the Polish economic environment, this turned out not to be such a bad strategy: the firm has been growing every year since it was created.

Which creates its own problems. In a political system committed to the public ownership of the means of production, whatever private sector exists – and in Poland at the time that Sportis was created it did not exceed 5 per cent of economic activity – does so because it is tolerated rather than encouraged. Consequently not only did Sportis, during those years, receive no support whatever from state or local government – apart from the ruin it was offered in Serock – but its growth actually had to be covert if it was not to attract the disapproving gaze of the authorities. The Polish communist party continued to view the private sector – particularly that segment of it that could boast foreign connections – as a breeding ground for spies and a hotbed of capitalist corruption, and for that reason severely constrained its growth. The Warsaw city authorities were responsible for granting Sportis its production licence and would only do so if it was prepared to limit the size of its establishment to sixty employees and get its products approved. The firm, however, in line with current practice elsewhere, would be allowed to take on part-timers beyond its full-time staffing allocation, a concession which allowed it to share some staff with another firm, Christine, created almost at the same time as Sportis itself and owned by Thomas Holç's British wife. Christine was a manufacturer of women's clothes and it employed production processes not very different to Sportis's and on a similar scale. There was clearly some scope for synergy between the two firms.

Continued growth and opportunities to diversify into survival suits and inflatable rescue boats led Sportis in 1989 to create a wholly owned subsidiary in the hamlet of Bojano, some 15 kilometres outside Gdansk and three hours by train from Warsaw. Production facilities are located in an extension of an old chicken hut and are reached by a dirt track. Ludwig Vogt, the director of the subsidiary and the inspiration behind it, had been a captain in the merchant navy and had spent time working in a testing station for sea rescue equipment. He had had dealings with Sportis for a number of years when acting as an adviser to the firm's clients and was recruited by Sportis largely on account of his detailed knowledge of customer requirements with respect to the products that the Bojano factory would be producing.

The choice of Gdansk as a location was dictated by the fact that expansion could no longer be sensibly accommodated on the Serock site and that labour practices and attitudes in the Gdansk region seemed to be more flexible than around Warsaw. What settled the matter, though, was that Gdansk happened to be where Ludwig Vogt happened to live!

SPORTIS: CURRENT PERFORMANCE

Sportis today finds itself in a radically different economic environment to that which confronted it at birth nearly a decade ago. The opportunities discernible on the horizon for many Polish firms following the collapse of the communist order, are now neatly counterbalanced by a number of looming threats that may trip them up long before they ever reach that horizon. The fog of confusion that currently shrouds the country's real economic performance is undermining the fragile consensus so necessary for the difficult policy decisions that lie ahead. Indeed, even western counsels are divided on the matter of how well the country is doing and where it is headed for. Inflation, at 5 per cent a month, is a great improvement over what it was in 1990 but with the zloty now pegged to the dollar, it remains a major headache for firms having to turn outward towards exports and now caught in a vicious cost squeeze.

Official figures on the Polish economy may make grim reading – industrial production, it is claimed, fell by a third in 1990 – but how reliable are they? Official statistics are designed to measure the state economy. Private industry, that shadowy army of under-reporting plumbers, carpenters, truckers, and small traders, is for the most part ignored. In a communist system in which the private sector was largely made up of Marx's 'petty commodity traders' and never allowed to exceed more than 5 per cent of national output, such neglect was understandable and probably not particularly harmful. Yet the Polish government's statistical office believes that the output of private industry (excluding farming) grew by over 50 per cent in 1990 and now – in mid-1991 – accounts for 18 per cent of national income, up from 11 per cent in 1989. And in the latter year, the government's statisticians guess, the number of people employed in private enterprise grew by more than 500,000, bringing the total to between 1.8 million and 2 million people. These figures merely confirm what casual empiricism thrusts before the gaze of all foreign visitors to the country today: every Polish town now has its street markets where everything from imported toothpaste to once unavailable Polish ham can be bought; the area around Warsaw's Palace of Culture, for example, has been transformed into a vast oriental *souk*. Queues in post-communist Poland have virtually disappeared.

Yet if many of these mushrooming small private firms are doing well it is because they have positioned themselves at the consumer end of what was an archaic state distribution system and have been able to respond as nimble traders do everywhere to pent up consumer needs. Sportis, as a production organization, by contrast, is placed upstream of the state distributors on which it has relied for a regular flow of orders as well as detailed feedback on what end users of its products required in terms of quality and performance.

The state distribution system on which Sportis was so dependent has now collapsed and it is of no consolation to the firm that its main state-owned competitor has collapsed along with it. Sportis is in the paradoxical position of being the sole domestic producer – indeed, with only modest imports in these products' markets the firm is virtually a monopolist – in a market to which it currently has little or no access.

The firm confronts this odd situation with no marketing organ-ization to speak of. Michal Syski, the sales manager, joined Sportis in 1985 but, until very recently, he has been the only person in the organization involved in the selling function. As he explains it, marketing as such was never needed under the old system. The firm produced to order and luckily there were always orders in the distributor's pipeline. Exactly where the pipeline led to had never much bothered anyone.

To build up its marketing capacity, Sportis has now recruited a salesman who reports to Ludwig Vogt in Bojano and whose job it is to contact retailers directly. This is proving more difficult than expected: retailers are hard to identify and in the current economic climate at any one time as many are going out of business as are opening up. They are thus a rapidly moving and oft disappearing target. A further complication lies in trying to assess the current level of demand for Sportis's products given income levels that prevail in Poland at present. Per capita income continues to decline, but no one seems to be able to say at exactly what rate. The traditional users of Sportis's main products are all facing hard times – deep-sea fishing firms in Poland are now selling off a large part of their fleets and many face bankruptcy – but with the reforms new market segments are also making their appearance, especially in the field of leisure.

Given the pervasive bleakness of it all the firm's sales and profit may occasion some surprise. On paper, at least, it does not seem to be doing as badly as its domestic circumstances would lead one to believe (Appendix 5.2 gives Sportis's sales figures). There are two explanations for this.

The first is that in the last year Thomas Holç has reoriented Sportis towards external markets as originally intended. In addition to a growing Soviet business, the firm has started manufacturing under contract for Compass, a Swedish firm producing vests and life-jackets for sailors. In 1990, Compass, facing rising labour costs as home, relocated its production in the Bojano plant and just held on to the design and marketing function. Bojano now produces between 120,000 and 150,000 pieces a year for its new Swedish client.

Sportis is also manufacturing under contract for Musto Ltd of Benfleet, in Essex (UK). Keith Musto, the owner, is an old friend of Thomas Holç from their sailing days. His firm, like Compass, specializes in protective clothing for sailors. He had originally intended to subcontract production operations to a Hong Kong firm but found the geographical distance too great for effective coordination. He then approached Sportis with a trial order, supplying it with both the designs and the raw materials. The firm now carries out six months' worth of production for Musto each year and a joint venture between the two firms is currently under discussion. Both sides remain cautious on this matter, however, for they agree that Sportis is not yet sufficiently cost effective to be a viable joint venture partner.

The lack of cost effectiveness hints at a second possible reason why the company's sales and profit figures look so good: the absence of an accounting system that can accurately track and describe the firm's present or past financial performance. Small private businesses in Poland were required to adopt the same socialist book-keeping and accounting procedures as the larger state-owned enterprises. True to communist doctrine, the emphasis was on what was produced rather than on what was sold, and performance was judged by the value of output rather than the value of sales. In state-owned enterprises, of course, whether the firm made a profit or not was not held to be of much account since any losses were usually made up by state subsidies. Furthermore the financial data collected was placed at the service of supervising authorities located outside the enterprises rather than of the enterprises themselves, with the result that few of them knew how to convert a morass of book-keeping data into usable accounting information that could serve as an input into managerial decision making.

Thomas Holç made a clear distinction between the figures that he used for external reporting – which usually showed either a loss or a small profit – and those that described the 'real' business, which he kept in his head. In the past, the supervisory authorities had required two quite distinct sets of books, one for the tax office and one for the state statistical office. Holç had little faith in the relevance of the data contained in either set of books. Yet the figures that Holç kept in his head and which he used for the day-to-day running of the business, as he himself acknowledges, were often themselves only tenuously related to its performance. Like most Polish managers brought up under the old system, he was unfamiliar with the managerial use of balance sheets, income statements, and flow of funds statements. These were documents that the firm produced – after a fashion – but it did so only for the tax office. They were never used internally. To keep track of his business Holç made use of productivity data in the raw form in which it was collected by Sportis's book-keeper: measures of the productivity of different work teams; measures of time use by the staff; measures of direct and indirect costs; data on value added; summary data on monthly production, and so on.

Sportis's book-keeper, a woman trained in socialist book-keeping methods – Holç himself would not describe her as an accountant in the western sense of the term – perceived her role primarily in terms of external reporting. She played a key role within the firm since only she was in a position to follow and interpret the myriad changes in financial regulations that affected the firm. She was quite happy to make available book-keeping data to Sportis's managers but only on a request basis and usually only in the form in which it was collected – indeed, who in the firm would know how to specify an alternative form? The result was that no one in Sportis was in a position to build up an overall picture of the firm's financial performance. Holç is well aware of the problems this could pose. A short while back, his wife's company, Christine, found itself in some difficulty when, believing itself to be profitable, it discovered that it had in fact been making a loss.

He also knows that to get the firm's productivity up to competitive levels he must quickly establish a better control of costs. Until recently, this hardly seemed necessary. Inputs, including labour, were cheap, and were of an acceptable quality for the domestic market. Unrelenting inflation and the urgent need to find new markets abroad have changed all that. The point was driven home when Sportis was visited by the US firm, Levi's, which was seeking out potential Polish subcontractors; in the course of discussions Sportis discovered that it required thirty minutes to produce a pair of denims that the US firm could produce in six and a half. 'They thought that they would make us feel better by telling us not to be too despondent since, after all, it had taken Levi's a hundred years to reach such a level of productivity', commented Syski ruefully.

The absence of an effective accounting system poses a more subtle challenge to Sportis than simply improving current productivity levels. With the company's growth and diversification – it is currently preparing to move into the production of oil booms based on the technology it is using for inflatable rescue boats – Holç increasingly feels the need to decentralize some management decisions. Some first steps have been taken. The sharing of staff with Christine – book-keeper, sales manager (Syski), production manager, deliveries, purchasing, and administrative staff, and not the least, Thomas Holç himself – was being terminated. Sportis would maintain its head offices on Christine's production site at Marki but from now on the two firms would be run on an arm's length basis. (Appendix 5.3 gives gives Sportis's staffing levels.) At the same time, Holç was preparing to decentralize day-to-day responsibility for operations in Bojano to Ludwig Vogt. Major investments and decisions on product policy would remain with Holç but the rest would soon be handed over to Vogt.

Yet since Sportis had no planning or budgeting system to speak of, and since most of the knowledge required to manage the firm remained locked in Holç's head, he wondered how the decentralization would work out in practice.

SPORTIS: STRATEGIC AND ORGANIZATION ISSUES

Given the new opportunities and challenges that it faces, how does Sportis see the future? Perhaps it would be more relevant to ask how Thomas Holç sees the future since he is the classic owner-manager and for the time being takes all the strategic decisions himself – Sportis is legally a 'single owner firm' and is not required by law to have a board of directors. Holç, as chief executive, nevertheless works closely with the sales manager (Syski), the head of the Bojano operations (Vogt), and the book-keeper, but he does so on a purely informal basis.

'Sportis is what westerners call a niche player' comments Holç, 'producing differentiated products for a specialized market. I would like to see Sportis expand but not by switching to mass production techniques. This would bring about more changes that I could currently handle: a move towards automation and capital intensive production, greater investments in machinery and stocks and, of course, bank loans. The current rate of interest of zloty loans is over 80 per cent. Who needs it? I am not seeking the quiet life, but I don't want to die young either. Except for a small part of our production sold directly to retailers – about 10–15 per cent of our total sales – we shall go on manufacturing to order.'

Holç recognizes that such an expansion strategy is not without its problems. The domestic market offers uncertain – although by no means negligible – prospects and while Sportis considers itself the most competitive (because the only) domestic producer, a number of the new distributors in its product markets are turning to imports rather than sourcing domestically.

And the Soviet market which Sportis began to investigate a year ago is also full of pitfalls. 'Many Polish firms were spoilt in their dealings with the Soviet Union', observes Syski. 'In the days of the centrally planned economy, selling to the Russians was a picnic. Everything was routed through a few large state trading organizations and all that a Polish manager had to do was to drop in and pick up his cheque. It was all routine. Today there are no more cheques. The main challenge is to find a customer who can pay you – in vodka, Russian bears, or black market submarines, anything at all, in fact, but roubles. Unsurprisingly there is a lot of corruption about. Over there at present, it's everyone for himself.'

'To do business with the Soviets,' Syski continued, 'it is essential to build up mutual trust. Too many problems, both large and small, have to be overcome for people to trust a complete stranger. Take, for example, our new joint venture with Murmanrybprom. We drew up a legal agreement with them, yet we know, and they know, that many issues will arise which could not be anticipated by the agreement and that once the joint venture has been officially registered – any day now – our dealings with each other will be guided entirely by the quality of our personal relationship.'

'In spite of such difficulties,' Syski then added, 'the Soviet market remains a potentially attractive one for Sportis given the fragility of the domestic one. An added consideration is that western competitors are now showing their faces in the Polish market and this can only reduce the viability of small domestic producers working on their own.'

He then continued, 'Given the Soviet Union's current problems, westerners are unlikely to show up there quite yet, thank God, and since Soviet customers are generally still quite undemanding – we are to them what the West has always been for us: an Eldorado that we can only dream about – our price/quality offering remains quite acceptable to them.'

Did internationalization mean anything more for the firm than the Soviet Union or manufacturing subcontracts? Apparently not. Neither Holç nor Syski felt that Sportis would be in any position to move into western markets for a long while yet.

'To enter western markets – many of them already saturated – with simple products like ours, would require greater marketing and organizational capacity than we currently dispose of', argued Holç. 'We would be dealing with new market segments sensitive to branding and fashion trends, and we currently lack the design capacity to respond.'

'We might stand a better chance in the more industrial markets for protective wear and inflatables, where branding plays less of a role, but there we often meet protectionism disguised as mandatory technical standards. Sportis already manufactures these products to established international standards, but many countries such as the US, Great Britain, and Germany, still insist on local retesting, greatly adding to our product costs and hurting our competitiveness.'

Given Sportis's current lack of competitiveness in western markets, the subcontracting work that the firm was currently undertaking for Compass and Musto was considered something of a sideline activity and not central to the firm's future business. Holç explained, 'Compass closed down its Swedish operations on account of labour problems such as recurring absenteeism and high social security costs. It transferred both its production and equipment to the Bojano site. But the firm really only sees us as a way of keeping down its labour costs. It does not appear willing to involve us in the higher value added parts of its operation. We remain a source of low cost inputs.'

'In fact, not *that* low cost' Holç continued, 'If our wage rates are low, then so is our productivity. For this reason it is still unclear that the joint venture that we are currently discussing with Musto in the UK will prove profitable for either party.'

Improving productivity remains the firm's major headache. It is caught in a major cost squeeze which it is finding hard to analyse and to deal with. Direct costs went up by 250 per cent in the first eleven months of 1990 – as of March 1991 the figures for December 1990 were not yet available – but productivity went up not one jot. Worse, the local authority that leased Sportis the Serock site for a ten-year period, now wants to increase the rent from US \$2 a month to US \$2,000 a month – and this eighteen months before the rental agreement is due to expire. But with the zloty exchange rate now pegged to the dollar, none of these increases in operating costs can be passed on to the firm's foreign customers.

SYSKI'S SOLILOQUY (CONTINUED)

As he entered his car for the journey home at the end of the day, Michal Syski sighed audibly. His thoughts returned once more to the Russian joint venture that he had negotiated.

Was this an advance or a retreat for Sportis?

From one perspective the firm was exploiting a competitive advantage by 'working with the devil it knew'. But for what benefit? Western and Japanese firms were not exactly queuing up to get into the Soviet Union and it was obvious why: earning an honest rouble there – or even better, an honest dollar – was proving to be more trouble than it was worth. Syski had heard that these same firms had also had their fingers burnt in China and for much the same reasons. Yet it seemed that South China was now over-run by small nimble-footed entrepreneurs from Hong Kong, all discreetly making money in out-of-the-way places, mostly beyond the reach of the Chinese bureaucracy. Could not the Murmansk operation be of the latter kind?

From another perspective, however, Sportis's move east could be viewed as an escape from the new challenge coming in from the West. The firm did not feel that it could be competitive in western markets – indeed, it was not even sure how much of its domestic market it would be able to hold on to if foreign competition heated up there.

To become truly competitive in the western market, mused Syski, Sportis would need to undergo a cultural transformation. People would have to pull together and cooperate with each other to an extent until now unknown in Polish firms. At present everyone just attends to his own job in the organization – perhaps a consequence of paying people on piece rate – and teamwork is virtually non-existent. 'We must be operating at least 40 per cent below our existing productive potential because of poor work-discipline and other work-related problems,' he muttered to himself as he drove off. But things would be hard to change without professionalizing the management. And how were they going to do that? Polish managers are all like Christine's recently departed production manager; if they are good enough to run your organization, they are also good enough to run from it and to start their own, and that is exactly what they will do. No amount of bribery or blandishments will keep them loyal once they get an entrepreneurial twinkle in their eye.

What changes to its organization would the firm have to carry out to attract and retain the right people, wondered Syski. And would Thomas Holç, the final arbiter of the firm's fate, be prepared to swallow them? Would Syski himself be prepared to?

APPENDIX 5.1

WZT

Sportis forms part of the small-firm sector in Poland which today (1991) accounts for approximately 18 per cent of economic activity. Some light may be thrown on the prospects of this sector by a brief description of the situation currently faced by a larger firm in the state-owned sector.

WZT is a medium sized state-owned firm located about 15 kilometres from the centre of Warsaw and manufacturing televisions and professional recording equipment such as videocameras. The firm employs 5,000 people and is currently being prepared for privatization in the second half of 1991.

The firm's sales and output figures since 1988 are as follows:

Year	Sales ($)	Output volume	% Black and white TV sets
1988	52 million	379.000 TVs	70%
1989	70 million	402.000 TVs	50%
1990	96 million	370.000 TVs	20%

WZT accounts for 50 per cent of TV sets manufactured in Poland and currently has 30 per cent of the domestic market. Its nearest competitor in Gdansk accounts for 30 per cent of domestic production and 25 per cent of the domestic market. Foreign competition, however, is increasing as western firms set up local production. One US/South Korean joint venture, Curtis International, is already producing 100,000 sets a year locally at prices that WZT cannot hope to match. Its productivity per employee is too low – about a third of that of Philips. The firm is clear that if it is to survive after privatization it has to find a foreign partner.

Joint venture discussions are currently under way with several prospective partners – Sharp, Sony, Hitachi, from Japan, and Siemens, Philips, and Thomson from Europe, as well as a Taiwanese firm – on the manufacture of video equipment and a new TV casing. These prospective partners are all seeking to build up strong positions in a rapidly growing domestic market and to use Poland as a platform from which to launch into the Soviet Union. None of them is in Poland to exploit low labour costs. WZT has maintained its links with its former Russian trading partners and is in the process of setting up a distribution network with private distributors in the western part of the Soviet Union. The firm, however, faces the same problems as western firms in the Soviet Union: how to get paid.

WZT perceives its main attraction to prospective joint venture partners to be its technically qualified staff and the domestic distribution network it is in the process of building up. Eighteen months ago, the firm thought of itself primarily as a manufacturer and owned just two retail outlets in Warsaw. It now owns eight retail outlets directly and has signed up distribution agreements with another 70 throughout the country.

Given its current product range and its technical base, the firm does not feel able to target western markets yet. If anything, the share of its output that is exported has been declining – 12 per cent of output in 1989, 7 per cent in 1990. Discussions with prospective joint venture partners have also made it clear that the kind of technologies that would allow WZT to be more export-competitive are not on offer.

In preparation for its privatization, the firm's top management has been changed. The old *nomenklatura* appointees have been replaced by younger managers – the new managing director, for example, is 33 years old and has no line management experience – although qualified people are not easy to find. This is hardly surprising when it is realized that an experienced research engineer is paid 300 US dollars a month by WZT, less than half of what he can earn at Sharp's or in the blossoming private sector.

APPENDIX 5.2

Sportis sales 1986–90 (zloty)

	1986	1987	1988	1989	1990
Total sales	278,300,030	162,579,541	348,879,482	1,053,822,169	10,650,296,550
Domestic sales	278,118,067	144,552,311	326,502,545	1,004,546,738	3,897,554,145
Exports	181,963	18,027,230	22,376,937	49,275,431	6,752,742,405

APPENDIX 5.3

Sportis staffing

Location: Serock	*Numbers*
Production (direct)	39
Production (indirect)	9
Administration	8
Total	56

Location: Boyano

Production (direct)	85
Production (indirect)	4
Administration	15
Total	104

Note: Some administrative staff work for both Sportis and Christine.

DISCUSSION FOLLOWING A VISIT TO THE SPORTIS PRODUCTION FACILITIES.

Thomas Holç, the owner of Sportis, initiated the session by commenting that workers in Poland today lack both motivation and skills and that middle and top management skills are scarce. Recruitment, therefore, remains very difficult in spite of 1.5 million unemployed. People are not willing to work and this makes it very difficult for Sportis to compete in international markets.

Asked by Lee Vansina how he controlled his costs, Thomas Holç replied that he personally monitored all costs daily but that all accounting figures were kept in his head; his knowledge of the firm's cost situation was of the intuitive kind.

How, asked John Child, does Sportis as a firm compare with its competitors? According to Thomas Holç, its technology is essentially the same as that of its competitors but its organization is quite different. The firm, however, lacks first line supervisors. Thomas Holç then reiterated the problems of motivating workers. None are really scared of unemployment. Official unemployment figures are misleading because they fail to indicate the extensive employment opportunities that exist in the black economy. Thomas Holç feels that the current attitude of workers is not conducive to enterprise growth and prosperity.

Lee Vansina felt that Thomas Holç was projecting a negative image of workers, a projection that could itself condititon worker attitudes and motivation. What effectively stimulated Polish workers, he asked, what 'turned them on'? Thomas Holç and his wife Christine replied that nothing did. For example, Thomas Holç tried to motivate his factory manager by taking him to England to visit comparable production facilities to Sportis's own. When the manager was shown figures indicating that productivity in the British plant was double that at Sportis, he assumed that the figures had been falsified. After all, falsifying figures has been a way of life in Polish firms.

Josip Skoberne observed that a lack of money could be pretty demotivating if wage increases failed to keep up with inflation.

Lee Vansina asked Thomas Holç whether he had ever dialogued with his workers in a spirit of partnership. He believed that changes in mind-sets at the base could only follow changes in mind-sets at the top. Tom Lupton saw this as a problem of changing and aligning divergent expectation, a long and arduous process.

Lee Vansina, continuing, felt that it was essential for Sportis to bridge the wide gulf that appeared to exist between management and workers – or more specifically in this case, between owners and workers.

Improving information flows within the organization and multiplying the number of feedback loops between workers and managers might help, suggested John Child. This would allow processes of positive reinforcement to set in, something that can be intrinsically rewarding if workers are given realistic targets and shown how to achieve them.

With regard to Sportis's external situation, the firm appeared to lack a proactive strategy, Max Boisot observed, and had allowed itself to be corralled into a subcontracting role responsible for a very small part of the value added to a final product. This led it to compete on the basis of costs alone with little prospect of developing differentiated products of its own and thus of expanding its competitive advantages.

Thomas Holç expressed some surprise that the Round Table participants viewed his continued attempts to cut costs with such scepticism. For his clients, he explained, costs play a primary role. Lee Vansina then asked him if there was any sense of partnership between the firm and its foreign clients. Do the latter participate with Sportis in the development of products or of manufacturing processes? Is there any evidence of commitment by clients to Sportis's future? Yes, in some cases, replied Thomas Holç, yet cost considerations still dictate the relationship between the firm and its clients, no matter how well intentioned the latter might be.

Max Boisot believed that Sportis's relations with its foreign customers were eroding its strategic autonomy. In a more proactive stance, the firm would be selecting its clients and not the other way round. A good client or customer is not one who simply pays his bills on time, but one who takes an active interest in the development of the enterprise that tries to meet his needs.

Ian Turner rejoined that in selecting clients one must be careful not to become overdependent on any one of them. A firm's autonomy is secured by the development of a wide and diversified client base.

At this point Thomas Holç asked participants to explain to him exactly what a joint venture was. Eastern Europe was awash with western and East European firms trying to set up joint ventures but none, it seemed, had any clear concept of the nature of a joint venture. Tom Lupton explained that a joint venture is an institutional pooling of risks and a sharing of rewards between two partners. Under such a definition, observed Max Boisot, Sportis is not really involved in any joint ventures at all but in straight subcontracting – with the possible exception of its Murmansk project. A genuine joint venture presupposes bilateral governance and a community of aims. Such a community of aims is not discernible in Sportis's foreign collaborations since for various reasons, the firm is being 'kept in its place' rather than being allowed to grow and develop.

Max Boisot further noted that some form of foreign collaboration appeared to be essential for Sportis in its current circumstances. Perversely, in Poland as in other post-communist countries, the ability to sell in western markets is a prerequisite – a badge of quality – for selling in the domestic market. Michal Syski commented that the domestic market for Sportis's products is currently in total disarray so that in effect the firm has no choice but to look abroad. Anton Artemyev voiced some doubts as to whether the Soviet market is really such a good place for a small firm like Sportis to prospect in. With hard currency trading now prevailing between Poland and the USSR, the latter has little reason to continue to buy the goods it used to purchase from Eastern Europe when for similar prices it can acquire high quality western ones. Michal Syski felt that Sportis could effectively hold its own in matters of quality. The key question was: would its quality performance register with a client whose mind-set remained oriented towards low cost suppliers?

Joaquin Muns added that there certainly seemed to be a quality prejudice in western countries against Polish goods and that therefore a small firm like Sportis inevitably faced problems in deciding which way to turn.

Max Boisot summarized the discussion by suggesting that Sportis needed to draw a distinction between a *survival* strategy – essentially a short-term response to current turbulence – and a *growth* strategy, which would allow the firm to develop. The first seemed to be pushing the firm towards cost minimizing measures and a concern with internal *efficiency*, whereas what the firm probably needed over the longer term was a profit maximizing approach based on competitive products and an enhanced organizational *effectiveness*.

A survival strategy would tend to keep the owner anxiously over-involved in the firm and its day-to-day business and would reinforce certain behavioural tendencies among managers and employees that he perceived as negative. The second type of strategy would place more distance between Thomas Holç's role as owner and his role as manager and would better articulate the managerial function at the strategic level. This, however, would require the creation of a governance structure for the firm in which the ownership, the directing, and the managing functions were clearly distinguished from each other. (See Bob Garratt's contribution, Chapter 1.)

Chapter 6

Case study four: The Barents Sea Gas Project

Jan-Peter Paul

INTRODUCTION

History and Geography have long made it elementary prudence for Finland to get on well with its powerful and unpredictable Soviet neighbour while nurturing its links with the more market-oriented economies of Western Europe. Ever since the end of the Second World War, this balancing act has helped the Finns to thrive. In 1991, however, the economic collapse of the Soviet Union caused the Finnish economy to plunge. The country's GDP was expected to shrink by 5 per cent by the end of the year and its industrial production by about 15 per cent. Will Finland pay the price for over-dependence on the Soviet Union?

In 1985, the USSR bought 21.5 per cent of Finland's exports; by 1991 the figure looked set to drop below 5 per cent. To make up for the loss, the Finns were desperately trying to keep trade going with a spate of joint ventures and barter deals. Their resilience and optimism survived the gloomy prospects. As Krister Ahlstrom, president of Ahstrom, an engineering group, observed, 'We've lost the Russian market before – in 1918 and 1939 – but somehow we always get it back.'

THE BARENTS SEA GAS PROJECT

The Barents Sea Gas Project was one such joint venture. Plans for this enormous undertaking were under way some time before the Soviet Union's economic problems were fully apparent. In early 1988, the Finnish company Oy Wartila Ab made a collaboration proposal to the Soviet Ministry of Oil and Gas Industry. The idea was to create a joint venture in order to exploit the energy resources that lay beneath the Barents Sea.

The motivation of the Finnish partner – several others were later brought in – was clear: The USSR was Finland's most powerful neighbour and the two countries had a long tradition of bilateral trading and collaboration. Finland had accumulated extensive experience of working with the Soviets in such diverse fields as the construction of nuclear power stations and ice-breakers, and thus this kind of large scale cooperation was not perceived by prospective participants as posing any excessive political risks.

Then there was the energy potential that could be tapped by the project. Apart from the Finnish interest in securing some of its own gas supplies through the venture, the area to be exploited was directly accessible to several important potential markets stretching from Murmansk and Soviet Karelia in the USSR to the northern parts of Finland itself, as well as Sweden and Norway (Figure 6.1). A second Finnish partner in the joint venture, Metra, had an interest in the procurement possibilities emanating from the joint venture, including that of acting as a general contractor for the supplying and buying of pipelines to serve West European markets. Metra is a major producer of building materials in Finland as well as in Estonia; it is also the largest producer of 300 kW diesel engines in the world.

The Murmansk Gas and Oilfield was designated as a first project for the new joint venture.

Both parties to the joint venture were concerned to create an organization that would be strong enough to carry out the field's exploitation with its own resources. For this reason, negotiations were initiated with other prospective partners so that by 1989, the prospective joint venture had expanded to accommodate the following partners:

Conoco Inc., USA
Norsk Hydro a.s., Norway
Imatran Voima Oy, Finland
Metra Corporation, Finland
Neste Oy, Finland
The Ministry of Oil and Gas Industry, Soviet Union

Soviet involvement, however, was in fact, more diffuse than it would appear to be from the above list, for in addition to the Oil and Gas Ministry, the following Soviet organizations were also to some degree involved in the venture.

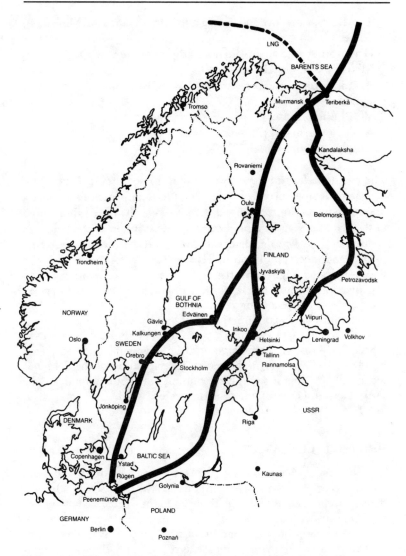

Figure 6.1 The Barents Sea Gas Project: Transport alternatives

The Bureau of Fuel and Energy (of the Council of Ministers), Soviet Union

Glavmornet (the main offshore administration of Oil and Gas Ministry), Soviet Union

Arktikmorneftegazrazvedka or AMNGR (Murmansk), Soviet Union

VNPI Shelf (Simpheropol), Soviet Union

Amige (Murmansk), Soviet Union

Gosplan, Soviet Union

The partners did not have to wait long to see their collaboration activated. In the spring of 1989, AMNGR informed them that a major gasfield, baptized Shtockmanovskoye, had been discovered in the Barents Sea (for a brief technical description of the field, see Exhibit 6.1). It was decided that this was to be the venture's first project and, accordingly, in March 1989 an agreement was signed between the foreign consortium on the one hand and a Soviet organization, Minneeftegazprom, acting as the Soviet partner, on the other, to create a joint venture.

A technical and economic feasibility study was then carried out to evaluate the new gasfield's potential. The study, initiated in April 1990 – one year after signing the agreement – and completed by the end of the year, indicated that exploitation of the field was technically feasible and that the economies of exploitation made the project a sound one. By the time the project would come on stream in 1997, a sizeable market would exist for its output.

PROJECT LOGISTICS

The major challenge facing the project as of mid-1991 was its financing – a challenge compounded by the Soviet Union's deteriorating economic situation and the perceived risks of investing in that country.

A two-phase implementation of the project was envisaged, topped by a twenty-year purchase agreement for the gas brought to shore. The first phase would initiate an annual production volume of 25 billion cubic metres of gas by means of an investment of US $10 billion. The second phase would then increase annual production levels to 50 billion cubic metres of gas and would call for a slightly higher volume of investment than the first. Joint venture partners contributing inputs to the project implementation process would be paid directly for these by the venture.

Gasfield

- Location:

  Soviet Barents Sea
  500 km from Kola Peninsula
  200 km from Novaya Zemlya

- Reservoir:

  Jurassic rocks
  Depth 1800–2300 m
  Good porosity & permeability

- Reserves:

  3000 mrd.m³ recoverable gas
  Some condensates

Environment

- Water depth:

  About 300 m

- Weather:

  Temperatures: + 23 . . . −27°C
  Winds: moderate, winter storms possible
  Waves: moderate
  Visibility: liminations in June-August

- Ice conditions:

  No landfast ice
  Drifting ice every 2 or 3 winters
  Small icebergs possible

Exhibit 6.1   The Shtockmanovskoye field

Just prior to the failed coup by party conservatives in August 1991, and the subsequent disintegration of the Soviet Union, the project was ready for implementation and preliminary work was about to start on the following activities:

- Environmental studies which would include a geological survey and an assessment of alternative routes for the pipelines.
- Further detailed financial and market studies.
- Seismological surveys of the field.
- An assessment of domestic sourcing possibilities in the Soviet Union.

This was also the time when final decisions were being made as to the joint venture's organization structure during the project design phase (see Exhibit 6.2).

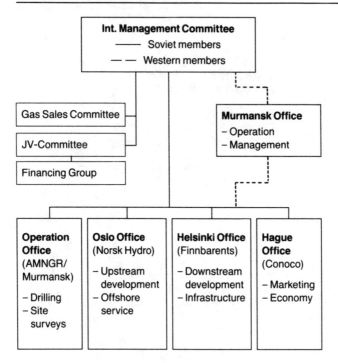

Exhibit 6.2 Organization of the interim and conceptual study periods

CURRENT ISSUES

One of the major motivations that drove the Finnish partners into proposing this joint venture was to develop further their competence in operating in the Soviet Union at a time when many prospective western investors were hesitating. Finland's extensive commercial experience of that country, built up over many years of experience, could be an important source of competitive advantage in future years if the Soviet Union unambiguously committed itself to the path of economic reform.

The failed coup of August 1991 had paradoxical implications for the prospective joint venture, however. If, on the the one hand, it made the commitment to radical and durable economic reforms more likely, it also heightened the risks of a total collapse of the economy in the short term. Furthermore, with the disintegration of the political centre and the devolution of both political and economic power to the newly independent republics, it became a critical issue to assess the future viability of the current partners to the joint venture, and to determine what their future institutional status might be.

The issue facing the Finnish partners to the venture is to determine the value of their extensive experience of dealing with Soviet institutions and a socialist environment in a world where these have been swept out of existence. This is an issue they face with prospective investors from the other ex-command economies of Eastern Europe seeking to exploit their historical links with their former imperial masters.*

DISCUSSION OF JAN-PETER PAUL'S PRESENTATION

David Parcerisas noticed that the consortium formula was becoming increasingly important in natural resources projects and the governance structure of a consortium with multiple interests was bound to be different from that of a more modestly targeted joint venture.

Jan-Peter Paul replied that in this consortium there was no one clearly discernible leader. However, since the USSR controlled the key resource – the gas – it effectively had the final say on any issue on which the partners disagreed.

Max Boisot, contrasting the experience of Jan-Peter Paul's company in the USSR with that of Sportis in the same country, wondered if the latter was not too small to operate in an environment as difficult and volatile as that of the ex-Soviet Union. Isn't there perhaps a minimum size of firm that can engage in cross-border operations when governance systems are not compatible?

Jan-Peter Paul replied that, in his view, operating in the USSR requires a long-term commitment and that it was likely that only larger firms were in any position to take on the risks and financial burdens of such a commitment. A long-term involvement is required not just because of the nature and scale of projects undertaken – in this case a natural resource project – but also to build up a basis of common understanding and good will essential to successful collaboration. In addition, only the larger projects – by implication, the

* The project has, in 1993, been put on ice. The international consortium has been replaced by a Russian consortium representing mainly the Russian state armaments industry.

ones undertaken by the larger foreign firms – offer the scale economies that would justify investment in essential infrastructure. Given the scarcity of everything in the USSR, without such investments in infrastructure – railways, roads, etc. – investment projects cannot succeed.

Ian Turner asked Jan-Peter Paul what might be the role of central government in such large projects. The latter replied that government involvement was indeed essential to clear a path for the project through the administrative and economic quagmire that prevails, but that many other types of institutions also needed to be involved to enhance the project's prospects of success. Such institutions, however, – a stockmarket, a commercial banking system, a legal framework, etc. – simply did not exist in the USSR today.

Summarizing, Max Boisot sensed that creating appropriate governance structures for the kind of collaboration described by Jan-Peter was but one step, albeit an essential one, in a broader effort in which institutional reform and development had to be undertaken on a wide front. Large-scale resources from abroad would not be committed to the country in the absence of such an effort. Yet, paradoxically, it might be that small nimble-footed firms like Sportis secure their competitive advantages in such an environment precisely by being able to survive and prosper in the absence of the kind of institutional infrastructure required by larger firms. By knowing the ropes and by having the contacts they can secure for themselves profitable operating niches that larger firms would deem too risky to exploit. If such were the case, he mused, then it was likely that the governance problems of the small owner-managed firm in the post-communist environment would be quite different from those of the larger firms. And since small owner-managed firms were likely to be an important source of future growth in post-communist Europe, it followed that more attention should be devoted to their specific governance needs.

Chapter 7

Host country managerial behaviour in Chinese and Hungarian joint ventures
Assessment of competing explanations*

John Child and Livia Markoczy

INTRODUCTION

Corporate governance does not operate in a vacuum. It is shaped by, and in turn, contributes to shaping both an institutional framework of industrial governance as well as specific cultural and historical forces. Separating out what is the part played by industrial governance and what is the part played by culture and history, however, is not easy. The line that divides them is readily blurred. One fruitful approach is to look at situations where industrial governance is across cultural boundaries, since this tends to bring to the surface issues that may originate in the way that governance is exercised rather than in cultural features.

Research recently conducted by the authors has found close similarities in the behaviour of host country managers in Chinese (PRC) and Hungarian equity joint ventures (EJVs). The purpose of this paper is to consider why this should be so. It begins by summarizing some of the salient features of Chinese and Hungarian managerial behaviour indicated by the research. It then notes several perspectives which purport to account for managerial behaviour in these contexts, namely those referring to the system of industrial governance, the level of industrialization, national culture, and the phenomenon of resistance to change. How far the behaviour of managers can be accounted for by cultural differences rather than those in the economic and institutional environment that they confront, and whether multiple and complementary

* This paper was presented at the third COS Round Table, held in Warsaw in summer 1991. A revised version has appeared as 'Host-country managerial behaviour and learning in Chinese and Hungarian joint ventures', *Journal of Management Studies*, 30: 4, July 1993: 631–51.

explanations are in fact necessary, are matters of keen contemporary debate (Hall and Xu 1990). The four explanations are then assessed in the light of the research findings and implications are drawn for theory and practice.

HOST COUNTRY MANAGERIAL BEHAVIOUR

The findings summarized in this section come from two studies. The first is an investigation of thirty Sino-foreign EJVs conducted by Child and his colleagues during 1989 (Child et al. 1990). These EJVs included manufacturing and service organizations, and had American, European, Japanese and Hong Kong foreign partners. The second is an in-depth investigation of five Hungarian-foreign EJVs conducted by Markoczy and her colleagues (Markoczy 1990, 1993; Szajko and Kata 1990). Four were manufacturing companies and one was a bank. The partners were American, British, French, and Italian.

Both studies focused on the managerial practices adopted in these companies. They relied on a combination of open-ended interviewing, access to documents and opportunistic observation. The findings reported here derive from the reports of foreign managers on the behaviour of their local managerial partners. Foreign partners singled out similar areas of local managerial behaviour in both countries and, even more remarkable, they mentioned key characteristics and/or problems in more or less identical terms. The main areas of behaviour concerned (1) decision making, (2) communication, and (3) personnel policy.

DECISION MAKING

In both countries, local managers were said to avoid making individual decisions and accepting responsibility for their actions. In almost half (13 out of 30) of the Chinese EJVs, examples were spontaneously offered of how local managers preferred the foreign partner to take the risk of blame in the event of failure in a given line of action. For instance, Chinese departmental managers in one company refused to implement decisions even after approval at a senior management meeting unless the general manager provided written authorization for it. Similarly, a foreign manager in one of the Hungarian EJVs commented: 'The Hungarians do not want to make decisions or take responsibility. If a problem is mentioned to you (by a Hungarian), it becomes your problem.'

The eagerness of the host country managers to shift responsibility and blame away from themselves had its concomitant in a search for excuses. These excuses could give rise to serious misinformation being provided to foreign partners.

The low defensive profile of local managers and their apparent deference towards authority combined to give rise to a passive mode of behaviour in meetings with foreign managers. In both countries, it was regularly reported that local managers were unwilling to express individual opinions in meetings. One Japanese manager recalled that in his Chinese EJV, 'When we attempted to set up problem-solving meetings, it turned out to be useless. The Chinese executives offered no suggestions.' An American manager confessed that, with reference to his Hungarian partner's behaviour in meetings, 'We do not know whether the Hungarians agree with the decisions or whether they are just good soldiers.'

COMMUNICATION

In both countries it was reported that local managers were unwilling to share information or, where they were willing, they provided information that was inappropriate. There were several aspects to this behaviour. Firstly, local managers consistently failed to pass information down to their subordinates. Secondly, communication horizontally between departments was extremely poor. Thirdly, foreign partners complained that they were often not informed of problems that arose, and that any information actually collected was not well suited to the requirements of internal decision making. In both countries, local managers tended to insist on being assigned strictly defined tasks which they then followed narrowly, again to the detriment of effective communication and flexible working practices.

There was heavy emphasis on written communication among the Hungarian managers, which included much bureaucratic form-filling and a recourse to formal procedures. However, the formats used for such work – i.e. balance sheets or income statements – had been designed for the convenience of the higher authorities rather than for the needs of the business. Cost analyses were of limited scope and accounting conventions followed could be quite unrealistic from a market perspective, as, for example, when the value of inventory was included in the calculation of profit. Written orders protected the manager who tried to follow them even if they were not rational for the situation. Written job descriptions also offered protection against potential encroachment on the job-holder's authority as well as against the obligation to shoulder responsibilities outside a narrow definition of the job. Hungarian managers did not particularly welcome the effort of their foreign partners to restore informal oral communication in the interests of speed and efficiency.

Written communication, mainly of two types, also abounded within the host country management hierarchy of Chinese joint ventures: (1) reports and records both for the enterprise itself and for submission to the many departments of the local and national bureaucracies to which it is linked; (2) signed written authorizations for action by the enterprise or its representatives. Both these forms of written communication have much more to do with satisfying external resource-providers and powerholders, and with protecting managers from personal blame, than they have to do with the operational tasks of the enterprise. As in Hungary, Chinese accounting definitions and procedures continued to be used which had been devised to suit the requirements of higher administrative authorities rather than those of running a business. So while there were certain differences in the nature of written communication favoured by local managers in the two countries, their importance in each case appeared to reflect their common bureaucratic environment.

PERSONNEL POLICY

All but one of the 30 Chinese EJV foreign managers observed a great difference between their home country personnel practices and those they were obliged to follow in China. Major differences were also noted by foreign joint venture managers working in Hungary. Particular difficulties were experienced in both countries due both to the absence of effective systems for selecting and firing employees as well as the absence of effective incentive systems.

Eleven of the 30 Chinese EJVs were able to recruit at their discretion on the open labour market. Others experienced restrictions frequently coupled with pressures from local labour bureaux to take on people indiscriminately without regard to competence or numbers required. In Hungary there had been an interest in obtaining slack human capacity and local managers had therefore been unselective in their hiring practices. This reflected a shortage of skilled labour and the peculiar practice of taxing enterprises on the basis of their average wage level. Unsurprisingly, managers were thus encouraged to hire low-paid workers in order to offset the favourable rates at which they needed to pay key workers.

Only three of the Chinese EJVs said that it was straightforward to fire unsatisfactory workers. In the Hungarian firms no procedure actually existed for firing people. In China, dismissing workers created a special problem because no safety net of unemployment benefits was available to them and the provision of housing is generally tied to jobs. In both countries, socialist ideology had for a long time asserted that everybody has a right to work and this had become a deeply rooted assumption in the minds of workers and managers alike.

The application of an effective rewards policy is vitiated in many Chinese enterprises by (1) the failure to differentiate payments according to level of responsibility and (2) the failure to operate incentives by relating bonuses to performance – instead bonuses are effectively consolidated into employees' fixed salaries. After some resistance, however, two-thirds of the EJVs were operating incentive bonus schemes, while 40 per cent of them had developed a differential salary system which endeavoured to reflect responsibility. In Hungary, bonus levels were related to the size of the enterprise rather than to its profitability and, until recently, possibilities for increasing wages were restricted by regulations. One of the most urgent needs experienced by new foreign EJV partners was the installation of new incentive systems in an environment where there had previously been little interest in encouraging the effective use of labour.

POTENTIAL EXPLANATIONS

The system of industrial governance

Economy and industry in China and, until recently, in Hungary, have been governed through a system of state socialism. This system is marked by the economic and political dependency of state enterprises upon higher authorities which, in turn, protect the specific enterprises in their care through subsidies and by placing restrictions on free competition. It is essentially a paternalistic system of political economy with two parallel (but intensively interrelated) hierarchies, those of the administration and the Party. In both countries, even today, most large enterprises remain state-owned and the state sector forms a major part of the industrial economy (Hare 1990; State Statistical Bureau 1992). Although

Chinese and Hungarian joint venture laws afford EJVs greater freedom from both direct administrative and political controls, the behaviour of local managers working in these ventures reflects how extensively they have learned to cope with the state socialist governance system.

The structures of industrial governance in each country were originally laid down on the pattern of the centralized Soviet model. They located the enterprise within a matrix comprising two administrative lines, direct and functional, leading down to state-owned enterprises. In Hungary the key state organs were, until the early 1980s, industry ministries which dealt directly with a relatively small number of state enterprises, themselves controlling individual producing units. These were subsequently merged to form more general ministries (Industry, Trade, etc.) which no longer exercised such close direct supervision over enterprises. In China, a far larger country, local provincial or metropolitan governments generally play the most important guidance and regulatory role. Under economic reform in both countries, functional bureaux such as those belonging to the finance ministry, came to play a more important role in monitoring and qualifying enterprise autonomy. In China, Party organs form a parallel hierarchy and are embodied in each unit of the structure described; it was only in 1990 that these were abolished in Hungary.

Three key characteristics of the relationship that developed between firms and their environment in China and Hungary are *paternalism, resource dependency* and *verticality*. For approximately forty years both in China and in Hungary, the economic and political environment was paternalistic. Initially, enterprises were absolutely dependent upon state planners and resource distributors for their existence. More recently, the state has learnt to regulate industry less directly through a judicious application of taxation, price controls, subsidies, legal constraints, and influence over the appointment of top managers.* The consequence of such paternalism was to locate state enterprises, especially the large ones, in a domestic market bereft of any real competition. In Hungary it created a monopolistic position for them in the national market;

---

* Although regulations in China since 1981 and Hungary since 1985 allow for the election of chief executives in most state enterprises, the influence of government agencies over their appointment appears to have continued. In one Hungarian firm, management chose to enter the joint venture with a foreign partner to preserve its influence over top appointments for fear that a new government coming into power in April 1989 would attempt to fill these positions with its political appointees.

in China, more often than not it created monopolistic positions in local markets or provincial markets.

Moreover, under this system, enterprises were highly dependent for their critical resources upon administrative allocators and redistributors. Basic raw materials had to be acquired through governmental agencies in Hungary up to 1968, and in China this remains partly the case today. Yet other agencies then had to approve the acquisition of foreign exchange, and, in many instances, investment finance. Enterprises have also remained highly dependent on government agencies for critical information on, for example, forthcoming changes in taxation. Through its decisions on subsidies, access to export markets, and taxation, the government could redistribute the income pool available to enterprises at will. When there exists no possibility of obtaining critical inputs from other sources, the influence of administrative agencies on managerial behaviour is likely to be very strong (cf. Pfeffer and Salancik 1978).

The appointment of enterprise chief executives depended heavily on governmental approval as well as, normally, that of the Party. Enterprise managers were (and remain) also dependent for the fulfilment of economic goals on the cooperation of workers, most of whom enjoy job security as well as a privileged legitimacy in ideological terms. They could express any dissatisfaction they felt in ways that would jeopardize management plans, such as by working to rule and refusing to cooperate flexibly in dealing with the myriad problems caused by shortages. Such managerial dependence was only partially counterbalanced by the dependence of higher organs on the success of the enterprise for a continued flow of benefits – i.e. tax revenue, incomes, employment, housing, as well as other contributions that the firm makes to the community (Montias 1988; Child and Lu 1990b) – that might bolster their own position.

Finally, the dependencies built into this system generated a strong verticality within the firm in the sense that departmental loyalties were as much upward as they were lateral. It was difficult, therefore, to engender interdepartmental communication and teamwork, and the external dependency of the firm did little to encourage a sense of collective managerial responsibility.

In such an enterprise, managers had to devise ways of coping with a high level of dependency on the environment. This was manifest in practices such as:

• offering as candidates for high ranking positions (especially CEO) persons who can secure critical resources by influencing resource allocators through conforming behaviour or the ability to bargain with them. Thus senior managers in both countries spent considerably more time and energy bargaining with higher authorities than in paying attention to the market (Szalai 1989; Boisot and Xing 1992; Lu 1991);

- maintaining a strongly hierarchical organization underneath the CEO to ensure conformity and to secure political approval, behaviours which were more important for the survival of the enterprise than were the ability to innovate and to compete economically;
- accepting broad social and political goals for the enterprise from the supervisory authorities, in addition to economic ones, as trade-offs for their paternalistic support;
- incorporating practices which gain legitimacy in the eyes of resource allocators for the enterprise and performing symbolic actions that please them – for example, the adoption of political campaign slogans and the internal structuring of departments to match and reflect those of higher agencies (Soos 1986).

In short, defensive, conforming behaviour will have been learned under a system where protection from censure and the securing of necessary resources both depended heavily on the maintenance of good personal relations with higher level officials and, to some extent, with political organs within the enterprise itself.

Implications of industrialization

Economists and socioloIgIsts have long debated the implications of industrialization for the organization of economy and society (Kumar 1978). On one side is the argument that industrialism has a 'logic' which stems largely from its use of science and technology (cf. Aron 1967) and which requires the 'modernization' of a society's competences and institutional practices for its successful realization (cf. Harbison and Myers 1959; Kerr et al. 1960). Clark Kerr, a long-time exponent of the thesis that the logic of industrialism will lead to convergence, has more recently identified opposing socio–economic forces at play:

> The forces most strongly at work are the drive for moderniza-
> tion, the intensity of competition among nations, the existence
> of common human needs and expectations, and the advent of
> common practical problems with common solutions. The main

barriers to convergence are inertia, inefficiencies, resource constraints, and the holding power of any antagonistic preindustrial beliefs.

(Kerr 1983: 86)

Central to this thesis is the view that successful industrialization requires the rational allocation and organization of resources both within firms and even more importantly within a market economy as a whole. This means that the character of economic management should differ from that in traditional or non-industrial society. Weber (1964) believed that management based upon and operating through legal-rational authority was of this rational type and enjoyed a superiority in basing its actions upon technical knowledge and modern methods without the personal or social blockages associated with traditional or charismatic authority systems.

Both China and Hungary are still industrializing in the sense of endeavouring to expand their industrial sectors and to make them internationally competitive. The argument implies that, by comparison with more advanced countries, their efforts will have to overcome:

- a limited pool of technical and managerial competence;
- inefficient market transactions;
- a particularistic and idiosyncratic rather than systematic approach to management in which personal affiliation counts rather than expertise.

Such features of their industrial system are expected to result in inefficiencies which contribute towards shortages and resource dependence. A state socialist order which pursues industrialization through central planning will restrict enterprise autonomy and thus arguably further enhance these constraints on economic performance. The industrialization thesis also implies that any persistence of pre-industrial cultures will contribute to these attributes.

National culture

National culture has been the favoured explanation for variations in both the attitudes and behaviour of managers located in different countries (e.g. Weinshall 1977; Hofstede 1980), as well as for many of the difficulties encountered in the management of international collaborative ventures (e.g. ECRAM 1986; Tung 1986).

The long development of Chinese culture under a feudal social order was largely undisturbed by foreign influence until the present century. As Fairbank has put it (1987: 367), 'the influence of China's long past is ever-present in the environment, the language, the folklore, and the practices of government, business and inter-personal relations.' Many commentators, therefore, endorse the view that this culture is a strong determinant of the ways in which Chinese organizations are managed (e.g. Pye 1985; ECAM 1986; Shenkar and Ronen 1989; Lockett 1988; Redding 1990).

The following features of Chinese culture which derive primarily from Confucianism are often singled out (cf. Lockett 1988):

1 the respect for age and hierarchy;
2 the orientation towards groups;
3 the preservation of 'face';
4 the importance of personal relationships.

Respect for authority favours centralized decision making. Chinese loyalties are vertical in their orientation, and reflect the high acceptance that Chinese people have of hierarchy. This exacerbates problems of poor horizontal collaboration and communication within organizations. The problem is further compounded by a collective way of working, which tends to be strongest with reference to the immediate work group, to some extent the workplace equivalent of the family.

A strong orientation towards the group will tend to present difficulties for the development of individual responsibility and of systems to identify and reward performance on an individual basis.

Individual initiative and the evaluation of personal performance are also likely to be severely discouraged by the significance attached to 'face', as are frank contributions to discussions or problem solving. The Chinese attach much greater importance to the views others hold of them than is true of most other cultures (Bond and Hwang 1986).

A particularly significant concept in Chinese culture is *guanxi*, which refers to the quality of a personal relationship outside an individual's immediate family. Within the context of business relations, the norm of reciprocity applies so that it is expected that one favour will at some future date be repaid with another. Mutual favours are performed and 'strings pulled' on the basis of the guanxi that binds people together both within and between organizations. The possession of guanxi with government agencies can, under conditions of resource dependency, become a necessary condition of the fulfilment of enterprise targets and the continued ability to pay the workforce what it expects. On the other hand, the use of relationships to 'go through the back door', as the Chinese put it, can undermine the legitimacy of formal arrangements and distort the allocation of resources according to rational economic priorities.

Hungarian history and culture was strongly affected by its embeddedness into the East European region (Szucs 1983). The raw material needs of West European industrialization encouraged the preservation of Hungary's predominantly agricultural features and resulted in a revival of feudalism in that country (Okey 1982). The key cultural characteristics of this peasant society were conservatism, the integration of individuals into an extended family and community, a highly personal paternalistic dependence of peasants on the nobility, and within the nobility itself, strong personal relationships based on mutual favours. These reciprocal relationships created the 'uram-batyam' ('my brother nobleman') world in Hungary which preserved the power of nobility into the industrial period and set an example of horizontal loyalty towards people of the same social category. Such a world survived the arrival of the socialist era, where privilege based on birth was replaced by privilege based on political orientation. Reciprocity among peers played an important role in the distribution of resources, and of high-ranking political and economic positions among 'loyal party members'. Changes to the Hungarian social order always came from above, on the initiative either of the Hapsburg monarchs or of benevolent noblemen (Hankiss 1983; Kulcsar 1986; Moricz 1986).

Hungarian culture favours hierarchical, paternalistic relationships both inside organizations as well as between them and higher-level resource allocators. Reciprocal relationships within the leading social group play a significant role in obtaining resources and in securing high positions for the group's members. This has resulted in a 'counter-selection' (Hankiss 1983) in which professional competence and merit have been subordinated to political association. A highly paternalistic environment leads many managers to expect solutions to be provided for them.

Respect for hierarchy and the importance of reciprocal relationships within social groups thus appear to be major elements shared by Chinese and Hungarian cultures, probably because they are both fundamental to the functioning of an agrarian feudal order. Although respect for age, face and collectivism appear to be stronger cultural features among the Chinese, personalized hierarchical values promote relatively passive behaviour by local managers who then respond to a paternalistic environment in such a way as to sustain dependencies.

Resistance to change

The phenomenon of resistance to change has been well documented in organizational research (e.g. Mangham 1979; Watson 1982) and does not require detailing here. Such resistance appears to be particularly entrenched in public bureaucracies where existing practices may have been preserved over a long time, where organizational members may be able to secure external political support for the status quo, and where economic pressures for change may not apply so urgently (Warwick 1975; Biggart 1977).

The pre-reform environment in which most Chinese and Hungarian senior managers spent their formative years was characterized by vicissitudes engendered by the system – such as changes in regulations and the application of personal sanctions – which would encourage conservative behaviour and attempts to ride out events. The decentralization process initiated by both Chinese and Hungarian economic reforms, however, implies that enterprise managers will in future be held more accountable for the economic performance of their units. Under conditions of continuing economic uncertainty this may engender a degree of resistance. The importation of foreign ownership and management into equity joint ventures represents today a more immediate pressure for change and improvement, resulting, so studies of resistance to change would predict, in defensive behaviour such as deliberately withholding information and shirking responsibility. In the absence of a significant power base available to managers, one would expect resistance behaviour to be passive and covert rather than agressive and overt. It is also possible, however, that some of the resistance behaviour ascribed to host–country joint venture managers could, to a degree, be specific to the formative stages of their joint venture operations, and thus provide little indication of more deep-seated attitudes.

ASSESSMENT

All four perspectives advance explanations which have some prima facie relevance for explaining the behaviour of Chinese and Hungarian managers in EJVs. However, the system of industrial governance and the corporate environment it fosters, appears to have the most immediate and comprehensive impact.

In both China and Hungary, the attitudes of most local managers have been shaped by experience in state-owned enterprises which were dependent on politicized governmental resource providers. The influence of the latter is still expressed through their powers to allocate, or at least affect, the allocation of financial resources such as subsidies and fiscal exemptions, material resources (in China) and personnel resources such as managerial appointments. Indeed, despite favourable legislation, EJVs continued to experience what their foreign partners see as an undue level of dependence on and external interference by state bodies (National Council for US–China Trade 1987; Felix 1990).

The avoidance of personal responsibility, for example, reflects what may be called 'collective irresponsibility'. Protective forms of behaviour have evolved because under state socialism any failures in the system were often attributed to personal sabotage; it was then a common practice to create scapegoats. The best way to avoid becoming a scapegoat was to hide under a collective cloak and to strictly follow formal instructions. Thus while Chinese culture in particular might generate an initial predisposition towards collectivism, it appears to be more immediately a response to the nature of the socialist system itself and for that reason it is present in *both* countries. Similarly, the frequent resort to excuses stems from the fact that the best way to bargain for resources in a paternalistic environment is to convince the resource providers that a given task could not be carried out with existing resources.

Two other considerations also point towards the system as an explanation of what is observed. First, similar behaviour is reported from enterprises subject to state influence in quite different societies, both socialist and capitalist. Second, systemic differences, or differences in the way that enterprises are coupled to the system, have a considerable impact even within the same cultural domain.

A lack of independent thinking and initiative, together with information and practices which do not serve internal decision making but rather the wider bureaucratic system, are reported as problems in other contemporary East European societies (Gutner 1990; *Economist* 1990). Czarniawska (1986) concluded that the paternalistic and highly controlling type of governance system in Poland, for example, did not encourage the formation of distinct organizational cultures at the enterprise level. And the literature on public sector management in western economies also points to the importance of the political–economic environment in shaping managerial practices. Public sector managers respond to pressures from an administrative environment and a coalition of interests that place quite different demands on them than those that confront private sector managers (Allison 1979; Harrow and Willcocks 1990). Further illustration of the difference is provided by the comments of a senior executive in a British public sector company which was privatized in 1987 (interview with Markoczy). The most significant changes that he identified following privatization were that managers now made decisions themselves instead of seeking instructions, and that a new orientation had developed towards the customer so that, for instance, reports on market conditions superseded those written for government departments and political committees.

The impact of system differences within the same cultural domain is also evident. The contrast between East and West German industrial practices, which have become highlighted since reunification, provide one clear example (cf. *Economist* 1991). The considerable contrast in managerial behaviour between the PRC and other Chinese communities provides another (Redding 1990). Even a phenomenon normally quite indicative of cultural values, namely personal work priorities, appears to change with the system. For instance, Shenkar and Ronen's (1989) comparative study of the 'work goals' articulated by Chinese managers in the PRC and those articulated by Chinese managers elsewhere, pointed to clear differences of priority in those areas – autonomy and promotion – where one could expect system contrasts in the degree of external control over decisions and in the scope of career mobility. Moreover, Chinese and Hungarian firms which are not so closely tied into the central regulatory structure exhibit forms of managerial behaviour that differ strikingly from those reported here – both more flexible and more entrepreneurial in nature (Kiser 1989; Markoczy 1990; Williams 1990). They are, on the whole, smaller firms operating in the consumer, high technology, or service sectors.

The centrally directed and relatively recent industrialization of both China and Hungary helps to account for at least two of our findings. First, it explains the limited competence of local managers which is a source of concern among EJV foreign partners (cf. Boston Consulting Group 1990). The relative recency of industrialization in both countries is associated with a scarcity of institutions capable of training managers and those in supporting occupations. The fact that industrialization was bureaucratically rather than market-led is also significant because the skills which the state socialist system encouraged managers to acquire were administrative in nature rather than entrepreneurial. They did little to foster the competence necessary to address a competitive economic environment. Several foreign managers in the Chinese EJVs held that the reluctance of local managers to accept responsibility was largely due to their self-perceived lack of competence. Second, recent industrialization is associated with infrastructural inadequacies that create debilitating problems for managers, such as shortages and unreliable deliveries. But these are also a product of the inefficiencies in the governance system itself, so that one cannot impute too much to recent industrialization alone; after all, similar managerial attitudes are also found in the USSR which has a longer industrial history than China (Grancelli 1988), and the Hungarian infrastructure is in any case more developed than the Chinese one.

The industrialization thesis mentioned earlier identifies the persistence of pre-industrial attitudes as a further influence on industrial behaviour, with particularism and deference to hierarchy being prominent among these. Here we touch again upon the role of culture, in this case upon the effects of feudalism which is of recent memory in the history of both countries (Bai 1982; Okey 1982). It is arguable that the legacy of feudal attitudes created a more favourable disposition among the population in each country towards the centralized and hierarchical governance structures of state socialism than would have been the case in countries which had long ago abandoned their feudal order in order to embrace democratic capitalism. It may be no accident that state socialism never took root in 'liberal' societies with a strong commercial and professional middle class (Moore 1967).

Our findings strongly point to resistance to change as an important characteristic of host country managerial behaviour. The creation of EJVs certainly placed host country managers under considerable pressures to change, and their observed behaviour was not untypical in such circumstances. Moreover, economic reform in both countries had created, in addition, a somewhat more dynamic environment and this in itself was disturbing enough for at least some local managers. Yet this explanation cannot be the whole story. The behaviour of host country managers displayed a learnt pattern of responses to the system environment they grew up in too consistently to be simply a manifestation of resistance to foreign methods or to economic reform. Similar behaviour has been reported in purely local state-owned enterprises in both countries (e.g. Child and Lu 1990b; Granick 1975; Lockett 1988) as well as in the Soviet Union prior to the introduction of any economic reform and EJVs (cf. Berliner 1957; Granick 1960; Grancelli 1988).

Our overall conclusion, sketched out in Figure 7.1, is that the system of industrial governance – in this case state socialism – provides the most direct and comprehensive explanation of local managerial behaviour in China and Hungary, but that it is, itself, also linked to alternative explanations. The nature of this linkage requires some comment that refers us back to the culturalist perspective.

A major theoretical divide within international management research opposes culture, and hence *values*, as one determinant of managerial behaviour, and the system of governance, and hence *relations of power*, as another. Our conclusion has been that the latter can account for the similarity of behaviour of host-country managers in China and Hungary both more *directly* and more *consistently* than can a reference to culture. Yet, system and culture are linked in certain respects. The cultural dispositions in both countries towards hierarchy and particularistic reciprocal relationships reinforce a paternalistic system. However, those directing the state socialist system were often highly selective in deciding what features of their respective traditional cultures they would encourage and what features they would play down. They preserved cultural values which they judged to be consistent with the system, such as respect for hierarchy and personal loyalties based on reciprocal relationships. Yet they attempted to suppress cultural features for which they had no use or found threatening to the system. These might include family ties, village community life and religious practices.

The relative recency of feudalism in both countries probably paved the way for the initial acceptance of paternalistic state

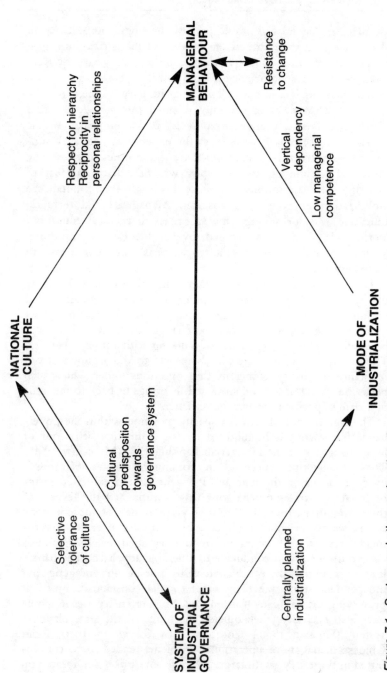

Figure 7.1 System and other explanations for managerial behaviour

socialism (by at least a sizable part of the population). Once in place, socialism then shaped the process of industrialization in a major way. Barriers to (convergent) modernization cited by Kerr (1983) – inertia, inefficiencies, and resource constraints – are directly attributable, in both China and Hungary, to the particular kind of industrialization centrally planned by the two socialist regimes. This was characterized by an undue emphasis on the development of heavy industry at the expense of necessary supporting infrastructure in communications and other services. The spread of telephones, for example, was held back for fear of fostering mass communications since this might then facilitate the mobilization of political opposition. Managerial and technical education was for a long time sacrificed to political education. Inertia was further encouraged by an ideological opposition to market and profit criteria, to material incentives, and to entrepreneurial initiative.

The general climate of uncertainty and threat engendered by the system itself promoted norms of managerial behaviour that encouraged resistance to change. Such norms are likely to persist even when the institutional context changes and may, if anything, be reinforced by the experience of working with a foreign partner. The key question, however, with respect to the argument from resistance to change, concerns the conditions under which such behaviour was learned and sustained. It brings us back to the issue of a firm's specific industrial governance.

The significance of a firm's specific position within the governance framework is highlighted by the distinctive behaviour of local managers in the Hungarian banking EJV (Markoczy 1990). They had effectively succeeded in avoiding the constraints imposed by dependence on the state and its agencies, and exhibited forms of proactive strategic behaviour that commanded the respect of their foreign partner. The relatively small size of the company and its service orientation placed it beyond the concern of governmental resource allocators and regulatory agencies. Its smallness and youth were also conducive to a flexible approach. The bank's leader exhibited these advantages to pursue an energetic and independent strategy which was *inter alia* consciously aimed at preserving the company's autonomy. Smaller enterprises in China have also typically fallen outside the scope of the state planning system (Hussain 1990). Complaints by foreign partners about Chinese managers or operational problems tended to be concentrated in those EJVs with larger Chinese enterprises and located on their partner's production sites. The effect of firm size and position within the governance framework may thus be common to both Hungary and China.

In sum, we conclude that the system of industrial governance has had a major influence on the behaviours that the host country managers of EJVs have learned, on the competences they have acquired, and on the way that they react to new pressures. On the reasonable assumption that the behaviours we have described can be taken as inimical to business effectiveness, two main policy implications follow from this analysis. One argues for distancing enterprises as far as possible from the residual institutions of the state socialist system. The other addresses the issue of behaviour change more directly, given that some of the factors conditioning behaviour in the system have now changed – particularly in Hungary.

First, foreign EJV partners should give priority to negotiating a genuine measure of autonomy for their companies from any external dependence on administrative bodies and, if possible, break the institutional and organizational inertia of the host company by establishing its EJV on a greenfield site. This may weaken the ties, real and perceived, between local managers and the system. Second, priority should be given to a substantial, but non-threatening, programme of training for host managers. This will not only raise their level of competence and resocialize them into an alternative style of working, but it is also likely to be perceived as a vote of confidence in their future contribution to the enterprise. Although investment in the cultural sensitization of foreign managers is unlikely to be wasted, our analysis suggests that attention to modifying the relations of host country managers with their critical environment and to raising their competence to cope with change promises more substantial improvements in performance.

While there is scope for initiatives of this kind, much will still depend on change in the institutional environment. Here one must be cautious. Within a centralized system, reforms that are introduced on a top-down basis will, of course, carry some weight, but their effective implementation relies on intermediate institutions and attitudes and good will at lower levels. Significant modifications in enterprise managerial behaviour require institutional changes which secure for corporate governance substantial autonomy so that, with Western help, practices can be reformed and new business relationships built up.

REFERENCES

Aron, R. 1967. *The Industrial Society*. London: Weidenfeld & Nicolson.

Allison, G. T., Jr. 1979. *Public and Private Management: Are They Fundamentally Alike in All Unimportant Respects?* Public management research conference paper, Washington, DC: Brookings Institution.

Bai, S. 1982. *An Outline History of China*. Beijing: Foreign Languages Press.

Berliner, J. 1957. *Factory and Manager in the USSR*. Cambridge, MA: Harvard University Press.

Biggart, N. W. 1977. 'The creative–destructive process of organizational change: The case of the Post Office'. *Administrative Science Quarterly*, 22: 410–26.

Boisot, M. and Xing, G. 1992. 'The nature of managerial work in the Chinese enterprise reforms'. *Organization Studies*, 13: 161–84.

Bond, M. H. and Hwang, K-K. 1986. 'The social psychology of Chinese people'. In M. H. Bond (ed.), *The Psychology of the Chinese People*: 213–66. Hong Kong: Oxford University Press.

Boston Consulting Group. 1990. 'Eastern Europe: The free market makes its debut'. *The Director*, 44: 115–32.

Child, J. et al. 1990. *The Management of Equity Joint Ventures in China*. Beijing: China–Europe Management Institute.

Child, J. and Lu, Y. 1990a. *Vertical Dependencies in Decision Making: Investment Decisions in China and a Comparison with Hungary*. Paper presented to the ECRAM conference on Management and Economics in China Today – Similarities with Eastern Europe?, Maastricht, November.

Child, J. and Lu, Y. 1990b. 'Industrial decision-making under China's reform, 1985–1988'. *Organization Studies*, 11: 321–51.

Czarniawska, B. 1986. 'The management of meaning in the Polish crisis'. *Journal of Management Studies*, 23: 313–31.

Economist (The) 1990. 'Perestroika – A survey'. *The Economist*, 26 April 1–22.

—— 1991. 'Investment in eastern Germany – Socialist paradise full of serpents'. *The Economist*, 26 January: 75, 78.

ECRAM [Euro-China Association for Management Development] 1986. *Chinese Culture and Management*. Brussels: European Foundation for Management Development.

Fairbank, J. K. 1987. *The Great Chinese Revolution 1800–1985*. London: Chatto & Windus.

Felix, P. 1990. 'Apporthintis: Vigyisvallalatok'. *HVG*, 8 December: 84–85.

Grancelli, B. 1988. *Soviet Management and Labor Relations*. Boston: Allen & Unwin.

Granick, D. 1960. *The Red Executive*. New York: Doubleday.

—— 1975. *Enterprise Guidance in Eastern Europe*. Princeton, NJ: Princeton University Press.

Gutner, T. 1990. 'Poland: Still waiting for the big deals'. *International Management*, (April): 26–7.

Hall, R. H. and Xu, W. 1990. 'Cultural influences on organizations in the Far East'. *Organization Studies*, 11: 569–76.

Hankiss, E. 1983. *Diagnozisok [Diagnoses]*. Budapest: Magveto Kiado.

Harbison, F. and Myers, C. A. 1959. *Management in the Industrial World*. New York: McGraw-Hill.

Hare, G. 1990. 'Reform of enterprise regulation in Hungary: From "tutelage" to market'. *European Economy*, 43: 35–54.

Harrow, J. and Willcocks, L. 1990. 'Public services management: Activities, initiatives and limits to learning'. *Journal of Management Studies*, 27: 281–304.

Hofstede, G. 1980. *Culture's Consequences: National Differences in Thinking and Organizing*. Beverly Hills, CA: Sage.

Hussain, A. 1990. *The Chinese Enterprise Reforms*. China Programme Paper no. 5, The Development Economics Research Programme, London School of Economics, June.

Kerr, C. 1983. *The Future of Industrial Societies: Convergence or Continued Diversity?* Cambridge, MA: Harvard University Press.

Kerr, C. *et al.* 1960. *Industrialism and Industrial Man*. Harmondsworth: Penguin Books.

Kiser, J. W., III. 1989. *Communist Entrepreneurs*. New York: Franklin Watts.

Kulcsar, K. 1986. *A Modernizacio es a Magyar Tarsadalom [Modernization and Hungarian society]*. Budapest: Magveto Kiado.

Kumar, K. 1978. *Prophecy and Progress*. Harmondsworth: Penguin Books.

Lu, Y. 1991. 'A longitudinal study of Chinese managerial behaviour, with reference to decision making, under the economic reform'. Unpublished PhD thesis, Aston University.

Lockett, M. 1988. 'Culture and the problems of Chinese management'. *Organization Studies*, 9: 475–96.

Mangham, I. 1979. *The Politics of Organizational Change*. London: Associated Business Press.

Markoczy, L. 1990. 'Case study of the Inter-Europa Bank'. Unpublished paper, Budapest University of Economics.

—— 1993. 'Managerial and organization learning in Hungarian–Western mixed management organizations'. *International Journal of Human Resource Management*, 4: 277–304.

Montias, J. M. 1988. 'On hierarchies and economic reforms'. *Journal of Institutional and Theoretical Economics*, 144: 832–8.

Moore, B. 1967. *The Social Origins of Dictatorship and Democracy*. London: Allen Lane, The Penguin Press.

Moricz, Z. 1986. *Rokonok [Relations]*. Budapest: Szepirodalmi Kiado.

National Council for US–China Trade. 1987. *US Joint Ventures in China: A Progress Report*. Washington, DC: US Department of Commerce.

Okey, R. 1982. *Eastern Europe 1740–1980: Feudalism to Communism*. London: Hutchinson.

Pfeffer, J. and Salancik, G. R. 1978. *The External Control of Organizations*. New York: Harper & Row.

Pye, L. W. 1985. *Asian Power and Politics*. Cambridge, MA: Harvard University Press.

Redding, S. G. 1990. *The Spirit of Chinese Capitalism*. Berlin: De Gruyter.
Shenkar, O. and Ronen, S. 1989. 'Culture, ideology or economy: A comparative exploration of work goal importance among managers in Chinese societies'. In *Managing the Global Economy III*: 162–7. Proceedings of the Third International Conference of the Eastern Academy of Management, Hong Kong, June.
Soos, A. 1986. *Terv, kampany, penz [Plan, campaign, money]*. Budapest: KJK Kossuth Publishing House.
State Statistical Bureau [PRC] 1992. *Statistical Yearbook of China 1992*. Beijing: State Statistical Bureau.
Szajko, L. and Kata, P. 1990. 'Organizational culture in G.A.' Unpublished paper, Budapest University of Economics.
Szalai, E. 1989. *Gazdasagi Mechanizmus Reformtorekvesek es Nagyvallalati Erdekek [Efforts to Reform the Economic Mechanism and the Interests of Large-scale Companies]*. Budapest: KJK Kossuth Publishing House.
Szucs, J. 1983. *Vazlat Europa Harom Torteneti Regiojarol [Abstract of the Three Historical Regions of Europe]*. Budapest: Magvbeto Kiado.
Tung, R. L. 1986. 'Corporate executives and their families in China: The need for cross-cultural understanding in business'. *Columbia Journal of World Business*, 21: 21–5.
Warwick, D. P. 1975. *A Theory of Public Bureaucracy*. Cambridge, MA: Harvard University Press.
Watson, T. J. 1982. 'Group ideologies and organizational change.' *Journal of Management Studies*, 19: 259–75.
Weber, M. 1964. *The Theory of Social and Economic Organization*. (trans. A. M. Henderson and T. Parsons). New York: Free Press.
Weinshall, T. (ed.) 1977. *Culture and Management*. Harmondsworth: Penguin Books.
Williams, E. E. 1990. 'The emergence of entrepreneurship in China'. In J. Child and M. Lockett (eds), *Reform Policy and the Chinese Enterprise*: 247–65. Greenwich, Conn: JAI Press.

DISCUSSION OF JOHN CHILD AND LIVIA MARKOCZY'S PRESENTATION

Imre Spronz commented that in Hungary, many state-owned firms have the strategic capacity to collaborate with foreign firms but are hamstrung by political constraints. For the typical state-owned firm, strategy equals government policy plus Party credo. Jozsef Menyhart added that a firm is more or less required to produce its own five-year plan which has to be in alignment with the national plan and is then translated into a series of one-year plans. The plan is its strategy.

Imre Spronz argued that in such circumstances, and given the irrationality of the plans, the core skill required of Hungarian managers is not strategic thinking in the western sense, but lobbying – of ministries, of Party people, and of bureaucrats in general.

This is the antithesis of strategy, replied David Parcerisas. In a five-year plan, especially as formulated by bureaucrats, there is no strategic response to the environment as such. The firm does not respond to changes in its specific product markets but merely translates – and quite mechanically at that – aggregated output targets as given in state and sectoral plans into a self-imposed quota. It does not ask itself how customers or competitors will react; its gaze is fixed upward towards the plan and the benefits it can secure from it.

Western firms, according to Jane Salk, thrive on information from their environment, from customers, suppliers, competitors. In socialist firms, feedback is not necessary to the firm's performance (John Child); indeed, in a certain sense, performance itself is not necessary or if it is, it is only so in a minimal sense defined by benign bureaucrats concerned to 'protect' their firms.

Joaquin Muns believed that in the West the extent to which socialist, state-owned enterprises lack the relevant information flows is underestimated; the same applies to the circuits through which information could flow, circuits that are considered essential to the proper functioning of an autonomous organization. Western observers tend to build up such firms in their own image and then become perplexed and frustrated when they discover that these firms work to a different programme.

Jan-Peter Paul wondered how relevant the lack of strategic capacity and the feedback mechanisms it required would be for joint ventures in Eastern Europe. Surely strategic thinking is the business of the parent companies that own joint ventures rather than of the joint ventures themselves? He could think of plenty of Western European examples in which strategic thinking in joint ventures is actively discouraged. Why should Eastern European joint ventures function any differently?

Summarizing, Max Boisot felt that if only one of the joint venture partners was doing strategic thinking, then in the long term this could only be at the expense of the other partner whose capacity for developing strategic skills would be impaired and who would then gradually slip into a dependency relationship. On a small scale, this dilemma was illustrated in the Sportis case where the foreign partner's agenda would always take precedence in any collaboration with the Polish firm because the local partner was unable to generate its own. The existing governance structures of joint ventures have no mechanism for safeguarding a partner's strategic interests if that partner is unable to articulate them for itself.

Index